HOME SWEET HOMESTEAD

Sketches of Pioneer Life in
Interior Alaska

Joy Griffin

Illustrations by
Shirley Timmreck

MADE IN ALASKA
3463

❄ Alaska Press
Anchorage, Alaska

▶ 1

Cover batik by Linda Rourke
Design & layout by K&H Graphics
Printed by A.T. Publishing & Printing, Inc.
Anchorage, Alaska

Diane Ford Wood, Editor
Additional editing by Susan Braund & Debbie Jamieson
Edmund "Ned" Wood, Distribution

Alaska Press

P.O. Box 90565
Anchorage, Alaska 99509-0565

A real-voice story of Alaska...

TABLE OF CONTENTS

PROLOGUE

Alaska
Fever

▼▼

It was madness. Up the Alcan highway we came, heading for a future unknown, with two young children in a half-paid-for pickup.

Anybody our age ought to have known better.

But Dick and I were newly, madly in love. That was all that mattered that summer of 1967 as we rolled across the continent from New York — hauling all our possessions — to homestead in Alaska.

I was a pretty poor prospect for pioneering. At 37, I had never dealt with life beyond a ranch-style house in the suburbs. My towheaded twins, Lanny and Dawn, didn't even know what Alaska was, but with seven-year-old optimism, they were ready to find out. Most of all, they loved their new dad and were delighted to be traveling toward a new life with us.

Dick — or Dad, as we have always called him — was nearly 50, and at an age when most men shunned change and dug deeper where they stood. However, I was sure Dad could do anything he set his mind to, and his mind was set on Alaska. Of course in my romantic state, I would have followed him anywhere.

So up we came, the four of us filling the seat across the cab of the truck. Up the unpaved highway in the days when people wrote "ALASKA OR BUST" in the dust on the sides of their vehicles. As the road stretched before us, huge clouds of grit formed behind everything that moved; it crept into each unsealed crack in our truck and between our teeth.

Then, through days of rain, we drove over potholes so deep that the mud splashed up to our windshield. The sweep of the wipers narrowed our field of vision to what lay ahead. It was just as well. The future was out in front, and there was no looking back for us.

Those 1,500 miles of highway transported us from the familiar surroundings of clapboard houses and cultivated fields to a strange, new world. As we drove through the great forests of British Columbia, the children were fascinated by the giant firs lining the road and towering over our campsites.

Then in the Yukon, tall timber changed to rangy spruce, bushy alders, and white-barked birch. With each new valley, I expected to see a farmhouse or two on the smooth, flat expanse of bottom land. But it was not farmland; it was permanently frozen, treeless tundra.

Dawn put it in her own words: "Nothing looks like home anymore!"

Along the way, outposts of civilization — gas pumps, tire repair shops, roadhouses — were situated at least 50 miles apart. Names of towns, written in bold black letters on maps, turned out to be stores with false fronts and real boardwalks.

A little apprehensive, I knew we had arrived at the last frontier.

Crossing the border into Alaska, we came to a "Y" in the road. Dad said to me: "Anchorage to the left — 300 miles; Fairbanks to the right — 200 miles. Which way do you want to go, Joy?"

Dad was serious. In this vast land, those were the only cities big enough to support supermarkets, Laundromats and department stores — places we would need to supply the homestead we would carve out of the wilderness — somewhere.

I'd heard Fairbanks had the warmer summers.

"Turn right," I answered.

We followed the road to our destiny.

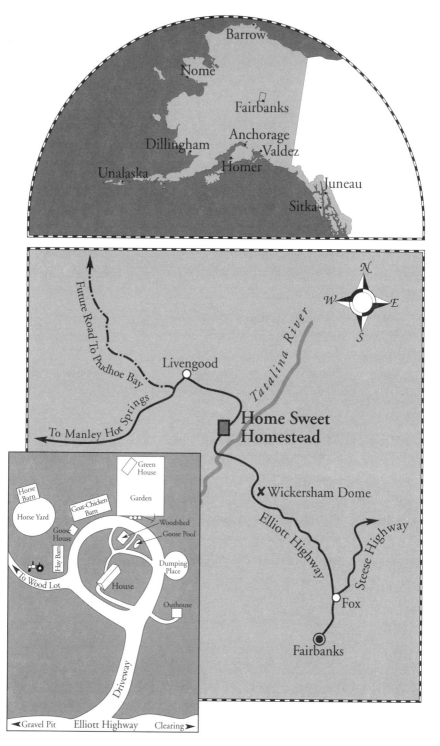

Barrow

Nome

Fairbanks

Dillingham

Anchorage
Valdez

Unalaska

Homer

Juneau

Sitka

Future Road To Prudhoe Bay

Livengood

Tatalina River

To Manley Hot Springs

Home Sweet Homestead

✗ Wickersham Dome

Elliott Highway

Steese Highway

Fox

Fairbanks

Green House

Horse Barn

Horse Yard

Goat-Chicken Barn

Garden

Goose House

Woodshed

Goose Pool

Hay Barn

Dumping Place

To Wood Lot

House

Outhouse

Driveway

◄ Gravel Pit   Elliott Highway   Clearing ►

ABOUT THE HOUSE

A Birch-Covered Hillside

A few weeks later, on a September afternoon, we drove out the Elliott Highway from our rented apartment in Fairbanks. We were on our way to the homestead site Dad had found on one of his scouting trips. It was on a lovely tree-covered hillside, he told us. The twins pointed eagerly to each birch grove we passed, asking, "Is this it?"

But Dad kept saying, "No, no, it's farther out."

After the first few miles, we met no vehicles, nor did we see any signs of human habitation. The narrow gravel road curved and wound its way through the hills. We passed many hilly groves, but when I, too, started pointing out sites, Dad said they weren't as pretty as the one he'd found. Besides, he noted, they were all too close to town.

Too close? We'd already been driving for over an hour!

I looked back on the days before we came to Alaska, when we lived in the East. From my easy chair in New York, I read about hardy families trekking into the wilds of the North to build homes and set up housekeeping — all with tools and equipment they carried on their backs. Picturing myself in their places, I thought how wonderful it would be — with a few refinements — to live such a life. But the heroes in my books had walked over woodland trails or paddled up quiet rivers to their homes. I was tired of riding over this bumpy, dusty road already. My romantic dream of wilderness life was fizzling fast.

Finally, we reached a wide spot on a curve about 60 miles north of Fairbanks. Dad stopped the truck.

"This is it!" he said proudly.

It really was a lovely spot.

To the left, white-barked trees sparkling with gilded autumn foliage towered over the hillside. To the right lay a broad river valley. The ridges of the hills beyond were tinged with hues of tawny gold and spruce green.

We got out of the truck and hiked up through the birches. As we climbed with the afternoon sun over our left shoulders, I realized we could walk forever in that direction. According to maps I'd seen, we would eventually arrive at the Bering Strait. If we about-faced and walked over the distant hills, we would come to Fairbanks. Or, if we missed Fairbanks, Canada lay just a few hundred miles beyond.

All of a sudden the vastness of the state, and the isolation of this tiny dot on a hill, unnerved me. I could not visualize home and family here. Where would the yard be, or the garden? There were no boundaries, nothing to give me a sense of place; we were just far away from any other place. My storybook pioneers hadn't told me about this aspect of the North.

After we walked around for a while — Dad with purpose and zeal, the twins with wonder and delight, and me with drooping spirits, we sat by an old log to rest. The children, already at home in the woods, happily explored the log's innards from one end of it. Dad took candy bars from his pocket and passed them around, yet I sat stiff as the tree trunks around us, my mind in a muddle. I'd honestly told Dad I wanted to live in the woods. But now, when it came right down to it — I wasn't sure.

In the crook of Dad's strong sure arm, I started to relax.

Then he smiled at me. It was a smile full of contentment, companionship and love. My heart did a flip-flop and overtook my addled brain. I knew that home was where Dad was, wherever in the world that might be.

Leaning against the log, in the crook of Dad's strong sure arm, I started to relax. I watched the sun shine down between a break in the trees and felt the ground; it was warm. I smelled the sweet scent of wild grasses mixed with the pungent odor of fallen leaves wafting up on a light breeze. I squinted my eyes and peered through the woods and saw glimpses of the valley across the road. If a few of those trees were cut down, the view would be nice from here.

Yes, I mused as I nibbled the chocolate, down there could be the yard; a big window might look out over it.

"Let's put the dining room right here," I said.

And that spot was exactly where our table sat, next to a long window overlooking the yard and valley beyond.

From that moment, sitting beside the log with Dad and the twins, this place became home to me.

Getting Started

▼▲▼▲▼▲▼▲▼▲▼▲▼▲▼▲▼▲▼▲▼▲▼▲▼▲▼▲▼▲▼▲

That first autumn passed quickly in our new homeland of Interior Alaska. By mid-September the leaves were gone, and in a few weeks snowflakes were falling.

While the road was still open, Dad made one more trip to the site to establish a survey corner. This step would allow us to file officially on a 160-acre homestead.

In those days the Elliott Highway was not maintained between November and May and, as the weather worsened, the highway became impassable. Without road access, we could not visit our land. So, during the winter, it lay unavailable and undisturbed under several feet of snow.

From the safety of our apartment in town, we watched for the onset of the "arctic severe." We waited for sub-zero temperatures and weren't disappointed. By Thanksgiving, the thermometer dropped to 20 below and stayed there. The sun rose late in the morning and set

▶ 19

right after lunch. At night the northern lights danced in the sky, and we stepped out to look without wearing coats.

We liked to believe we were toughening up.

In January, the temperature plummeted. We learned fast that "minus 50" felt much colder than "minus 20," and that "65 below" was worst of all.

Regardless of the cold, Dad drove to work at his swing shift security job at a satellite tracking site nearby. The children (unless it was more than 50 below), bundled up and headed for the school bus.

Fairbanks was often smothered in ice fog. As if nature wasn't challenge enough, the stinky, frozen dregs of smoke and automobile exhaust made us choke and cough. Crossing the street was life-threatening: If a car didn't have its lights on, it was impossible to see in the fog. How then, in the reverse, could drivers see pedestrians? It was safer to stay home.

We learned a lot about coping with cold weather that year. Warm felt- or sheepskin-lined boots were a necessity. Going without mittens meant frostbite in a hurry. Wearing no hats meant too much heat would escape from our bodies.

We also knew the importance of carrying emergency gear in the truck. One family we heard about spent many hours sitting in a broken-down car at 70 below until someone found them. They survived by huddling under blankets and sleeping bags they carried in the trunk. We realized that being knowledgeable about cold weather was a life-and-death matter in Alaska.

By Valentine's Day, the terrible cold spell had broken, and the days grew noticeably longer. We gained up to 14 minutes of light every day, and the sun was so bright it felt almost warm — especially as it shone in the windows of the truck when we were out driving.

Dad was becoming impatient to get to work on the cabin.

In the third week of February, fate intervened. A large Air Force plane made a forced landing on the Elliott Highway's right-of-way — about 20 miles beyond our homestead. In an emergency measure, the highway department plowed out to the site to cart the downed plane back to the air base near Fairbanks.

The road was open!

Dad's days off were in the middle of the week, so by Wednesday, we were on our way.

The road was in pretty poor shape; it wasn't meant for civilians yet. But the trip was a delight. The countryside was a winter wonderland — white and pure. A fox crossed in front of our truck and ran into the woods. Farther on, we scattered a flock of ptarmigan. This time, I was excited to be going to our homestead.

When we reached the wide curve in the road by our land, Dad parked as close as he could to the snow berm. We got out of the truck and put on our snowshoes. The birches glistened in the sunlight, and the air was absolutely still.

"It seems a shame to mark up this smooth snow with our tracks," I whispered as we climbed the hill to our cabin site.

Dad reconnoitered and I, with female nesting instinct, dug a big hole with my snowshoe, gathered some bark and twigs, and started a campfire in the bottom of the hole. I melted snow for tea in a fruit can with a wire handle hung over the fire — just like a pioneer.

We sat in the hole on snowshoe seats, dunking our tea bags and nibbling on cookies, making plans, and feeling very contented.

"Next time we come, we'll stake out the four corners of the cabin and shovel out the snow in the middle," said Dad.

"After that, we'll build cribbing for the base logs and put the walls up. I can get plenty of logs from the spruce grove up the hill."

Finally, it was time to build our cabin, clear our land, and settle down to homesteading. I still wasn't sure how we'd manage all these things — but I would find out when the time came.

Lay of
the Land

▼▼▼▼▼▼▼▼▼▼▼▼▼▼▼▼▼▼▼▼▼▼▼▼▼▼▼▼▼▼▼▼▼▼▼

In the years before World War II, Fairbanks was a small, two-bit town, a leftover from the gold rush days. In the '40s, the town came into its own; the military moved in and built Ladd Field, later known as Fort Wainwright.

Sixty miles north of Fairbanks, our homestead land was just a spot in the wilderness then. Once the far edges of the Athapaskan Minto Indian hunting grounds, it had become federally-owned and unsurveyed land. The only way to get to it was over an old wagon trail leading to the Livengood gold camps — a four or five day trip from Fairbanks. But soon, the Alcan Highway was cut, followed by roads that led out from town including the Elliott Highway.

When we arrived in the summer of 1967, our would-be 160-acres were still federally owned and open to home-steading. As we explored and hiked the land, we passed through a broad clearing; we thought we could detect faint ruts going through it. Were these remnants of the old wagon trail?

On the far side of a gully, we found the dilapidated remains of two tiny cabins, their roofs caved in, and alders growing up through them. They made us ponder who had been there before.

Farther on, we found another small cabin in much better condition. It contained a table, springs from an iron cot, and what was left of an old sheet metal stove. The walls were lined with flattened tin cans, presumably to keep out the wind. Next to the door opening was a hole in the wall big enough to peek through — or to fit a shotgun barrel. Could this have been for marauding bears?

Not far from the cabin, hanging on a tree, we discovered a couple dozen steel traps, long unused, sized for marten, lynx and wolves. I could visualize the trapper, resigned to his solitude, eking out an existence though the winter's cold.

These were our only clues to what had gone before. Except for a small gravel pit dug by the state, these were the few signs of human habitation marking the landscape.

Generally, our homestead left its history to our imaginations. But that made it all the more interesting to us.

Moving Things

▼▼▼▼▼▼▼▼▼▼▼▼▼▼▼▼▼▼▼▼▼▼▼▼▼▼▼▼▼▼▼▼▼▼▼▼

*P*uff, puff. *Whew!* I stood in four feet of snow, leaning on my shovel. I was never going to get this cabin site cleared. At the rate I was  going, the sun would melt the snow before I was through.

By the time Dad snowshoed down from the spruce grove with his chainsaw, ready to go home, I was more than ready myself. Neither my back nor my arms had any strength left in them. The next day, I could hardly stand up. So Dad drove out alone and finished the shoveling himself.

On our weekly trips to the homestead that March, it seemed that much of our work consisted of moving things from one place to another. We cleared the snow to make room for the log cribbing. Dozens of spruce logs cut by Dad had to be pulled from their stumps and carried to the building site.

Dad and I tried to drag the first log with a log carrier — a long pole equipped with a grapple in the middle — but after a few steps, I cried out, "It's too heavy!"

"Well, we have to get these logs down some way," Dad said, perplexed.

The next day, he brought along a crowbar, and a tool used to stretch fences called a "come-along."

We hiked up the hill to the wood lot and found the burdensome log. Dad wrapped the come-along's cable around the butt of the log. Then he secured the contraption to a stout tree down the hill.

"Now, let's see if this works," he said, manipulating the handle. The log started to move, but in a moment, the butt end got caught on a stump and he had to use a crowbar to free it.

"Okay," he said to me. "You try it."

I took the handle and pumped. The log slithered down the hill, inch by slow inch, with pauses for Dad to lift it over obstacles.

"Mama, it's going to take all the days of spring and summer to get the logs down this way," he said, frustrated.

He pondered the problem after we got back to town. By the next day, he came up with a solution. He built an old-fashioned windlass winch with a long spruce handle for leverage, and a thick spruce-log barrel to wind 50 feet of heavy rope onto. The next week he set it up, anchoring it to another stout tree 50 feet downhill from the stubborn log.

"All right," he called, standing with crowbar in hand after tying the rope to the log. "Start pulling."

This time, the handle was easy to turn and the log advanced foot by foot, 50 feet at a time.

We were in business at last!

Everything we brought to the land had to be hauled up the hill — chainsaw, gas, sledgehammer, axe; ropes, chains, peavies, drawshaves; a gas stove, water jugs, food, extra gloves, and toilet paper. Life's little necessities took on formidable dimensions when piled high on an eight-foot toboggan. We trudged up and down our well-packed trail.

Better do it now, we thought. When the snow melted, we'd be carrying things on our backs.

▼▼▼

One day in April, the whole family went to the homestead with a load of 12- and 16-foot floorboards. We had hoped to beat the spring thaw, but we'd had a spell of warm weather. By the time we arrived with 500 feet of lumber to unload, things were softening up. We started carrying the boards one at a time up the hill, but without our cumbersome snowshoes, the trail wouldn't support our weight.

We needed a bridge.

Lanny stumbled in the soft snow for the third or fourth time, and shouted, "Hey, Dad — we need a bridge!"

"That's not such a bad idea!" answered Dad, his eyes lighting up.

So we made one.

Placing one board lengthwise along the path, we carried another board to its end, and laid that down in front of it.

Then, we went back for a third one, and so forth, until we had a 500-foot-long bridge. Then all we had to do was walk back over the "bridge" to pick up the first board and carry it up the hill. Pretty soon, all the lumber was stacked in a neat pile by the cabin site.

▼▼▼

In May, we got ready to move from town to the homestead. It was important to start our residency on the land as prescribed by homestead law. We withdrew the children from school; we would be spending every night on our hillside.

Dad used the materials we had carted up the hill to build a temporary living place behind the cabin site. First, he put together a couple of 12-by-12 platforms. We put up our tents and sleeping bags on one, and on the other we set up a kitchen.

With summer still around the corner, we needed heat. So Dad spent one morning making an oil-drum stove with a smoke pipe on one end, and a tin door on the other. He flattened one side for a cooking surface, banging away at it with a sledgehammer; the forest resounded with the noise.

"We're here! We're here!" it echoed through the trees.

Every afternoon, we rode into town with Dad when he went to work. At the apartment, we packed clothes, canned goods, dishes, and pots and pans to use on our homestead. When Dad's shift was over, he picked us up and we drove the highway by the light of the midnight sun.

Within a week, we were moved into our temporary shelters on the two platforms. Our home looked beautiful to us in its lovely pristine setting. It seemed more like a palace than a camp. We felt like a royal family as we sat on folding canvas stools and looked out over our 160-acres. At least it would be ours, in time, when we met all the homesteading requirements.

The Dream
Becomes Ours

▼▼▼▼▼▼▼▼▼▼▼▼▼▼▼▼▼▼▼▼▼▼▼▼▼▼▼▼▼▼▼▼▼▼▼▼

While I never believed my life would evolve as it did, Dad was destined to become a homesteader. The first born of seven children, Dick grew up in the back country of upstate New York, surrounded by woods and wild game. At an early age, he learned to wield an axe and shoot a rifle.

At age eleven, Dick hired out to local farmers on a live-in basis. In those Depression years, the two dollars a week he earned made the difference in keeping his family fed.

Dick (and whatever farmer he was working for) would ride to the fields in a wagon, work with horse drawn plows and mowers, and load hay with pitchforks. At noontime, they'd get out their "lard pails" and have lunch — salt pork and cold potatoes. Morning and evening, they milked the cows by hand.

Most of the farmers were good to Dick. One sang songs and told him stories of the old days. The farmer's wife asked Dick to read on a swing in the yard on Sundays to show the neighbors he didn't work on the Sabbath.

Others farmers were less amiable.

One never served milk at the table; he saved every drop to sell to the milk plant. Dick was not allowed to use an oil lamp at bedtime in his small, dark room.

In his own way, Little Dick got even. He discovered a crock of honey in his room and ate from it every night until it was gone. Then he went over the hill and headed home.

Growing up, Dick's favorite times were hiking through the woods with his hunting rifle and fishing in nearby lakes and streams. Nature was his best companion; putting food on the table his reward. At sixteen, he joined the Civilian Conservation Corps, a government group that created jobs during the Depression. There he learned road-building with a pick and shovel, and carpentry with a hammer and saw. Then, he went to work as a lumberjack in the woods and, after that, he spent a few years in the Army's field artillery before rejoining the everyday world.

Deep in his heart, Dad always longed to return to the simple, down-to-earth life of his youth. Someday, he hoped to build a cabin in the woods and do all the things he loved to do.

▼▼▼

Meanwhile, I grew up in a far off world of relative comfort. Focussing on summer camps, city life, and school activities, I took most things for granted. I entered what I called "maturity" without a care in the world. My favorite things were parties, cigarettes and dry martinis, and I had no particular goals in life. It wasn't until I met Dad that I discovered I could do more than I ever imagined.

When our two worlds finally collided, Dad was the immovable object. He was stable, steady, and full of old-fashioned common sense. That spelled security to me, and as I spun toward him, I latched on and held on for dear life.

▼▼▼

Sitting around in the spring woods, we were happy with each other and enraptured with our little camp on the hillside. Lanny and Dawn were just as pleased — they knew this was their project, too.

Dad had followed his dream, and we had tagged along.

Now it was our dream, too.

The Tomato Soup Table

C abin-building time!

That spring and summer, Dad worked on the cabin each morning before going to town. With Lanny standing faithfully at his side, Dad could lay a log a day. I sometimes watched in fascination as Dad's skillful, capable hands cut, trimmed and fitted each log into place. Careful and precise, he worked steadily without a break. The rest of us all peeled logs when Dad needed them. We sat astride them, one person on each  end, as we sliced off long strips of bark with drawshaves. We became quite proficient workers ourselves.

We still slept on the platforms behind the construction site, but much of our free time was spent in the canvas-covered kitchen. We ate around a board table built into the corner — just big enough for four plates and cups. From there, we could reach anything on my rough lumber kitchen shelf without getting up.

We used a gas stove to boil coffee and make oatmeal, but most of the other cooking was done on the oil-drum stove. My iron frying pan fit perfectly across the stove's flattened-out surface. Dawn and I experimented with a small, portable tin oven. She made cookies, baking three at a time on a pie plate. I blundered through breadmaking, kneading dough, slapping at mosquitoes which always seemed to fall into the mixture.

When the long days of summer came upon us, temperatures rose to the 70s and 80s, and it was wonderful to be living outdoors. By this time, we were getting a lot of company. Some visitors came to take part in our wilderness experience, peeling logs, and trying to help Dad who would finally stop what he was working on to visit.

Others came to look at this odd family who had turned their backs on the advantages of civilization to move to the boonies. They offered advice on life in general and wrinkled their noses at the size of our cabin. They all ended up, however, around the coffee pot in our makeshift kitchen.

Later, dinner was served under the trees on a sheet of plywood which doubled as a table.

▼▼▼

Finally, one morning, Dad said, "I need the lumber from the platforms to lay the floor upstairs."

Dawn and I got to work, rolling up the sleeping bags and tossing them from the platform into the back window of the partially finished cabin. Then we retrieved our duffel bags and boxes as Dad and Lanny set up the tents in our would-be living room.

Next, we moved the gas stove to the top of an empty 55-gallon drum, and the barrel stove next to a window opening. Dad fitted the smoke pipe with several odd-angled elbows so it would reach outside and extend to the top of the house. Then we brought in the kitchen utensils, foodstuffs, and other belongings.

It was lunchtime; time for Dad to get ready for the drive to work. I started to heat a can of tomato soup as Dawn got out the dishes and spoons.

Realizing the old board table had been dismantled in the move, Dawn exclaimed, "We don't have a table to eat at!"

Hastily, Dad and Lanny nailed a half-piece of plywood to four leftover log ends. By the time the soup was hot, the new table was in place by the dining room window opening, and Dawn and I had set the lunch out on it.

We used this makeshift table for several years — covered with anything from red vinyl to my best lace cloth — serving food to family and friends.

It would always be called "The Tomato Soup Table."

The Tomato Soup Table

Bath in
a Teacup

"We'd better get water today," Dad would say. With that pronouncement, we all got ready to go.

For drinking water, Dad stopped each night at a spring near town to fill several jugs. But other than melted snow, the river was by far our best source of utility water. The tiny stream running through our homestead was impractical to draw water from, and our attempt at digging a well also had proved a failure.

So, in nice weather, one of our favorite tasks was to travel five miles to the river to fill our 55-gallon drums. Near the large parking area was a picnic table, and beyond that, a fishermen's path. A trail led through lush wild roses to a highbush cranberry patch. It was a very pleasant spot.

We had a pretty good setup for getting water. Dad hooked an electric pump to the truck battery; and Lanny stretched garden hoses between the pump and the river, and onto the drums on the pickup bed.

Each drum took about 12 minutes to fill, which left us plenty of time for play. Our only responsibility was to transfer the hose to the next empty barrel before the current one overflowed.

In the meantime, Dawn and I would spread a picnic lunch on the table. After we ate, we'd fish along the bank, pick berries, or just sit and smell the roses. We were never quite ready to leave when the last drum was filled and it was time to pack up and go.

Back home, Dad and Lanny unloaded the water by siphoning. The first drumfull went into buckets and tubs to be used right away. They stored the rest in empty drums set on pallets for later.

We used water conservatively. Every cupful had to be dipped or poured from something. Warm water was heated on the stove in a kettle. We washed dishes twice a day and, when they were done, we used the rinse water for other cleaning chores.

We were all experts at the wash basin; Dad said we were like his grandma — we could take a bath in a tea cup.

The gardens we would grow would have to fend for themselves: If the plants weren't tough enough to survive without sprinkling, they would not be homestead hardy.

I guess we all turned out to be homestead hardy. We became so careful with water, that we were abashed at how much other people wasted. That crystal clear liquid was precious stuff; we appreciated every drop.

A Kids' World

▼▼▼

I cannot describe our euphoria as the cabin took shape. The fact that it was built mostly of natural materials from the forest around us brought us a good deal of satisfaction. No architect, no zoning official, no outsider at all told Dad how to design and construct our new home. He often had to use his ingenuity, using irregular measurements and old-fashioned hand tools.

He worked on the cabin every minute that he was home. Of course, it was something he had dreamed of doing ever since he was a kid; he was having an awfully good time — and so were we.

When we became a family, Lanny and Dawn knew right away that they were an integral part of it. They had no doubt that their jobs, their ideas, and their enthusiasm were essential to creating this homestead. One reason they were so enthusiastic was that we rarely said no to their ideas. They learned by experience what would work and what wouldn't. They understood that this wasn't Mom and Dad's homestead; it belonged to the whole family.

Lanny and Dawn had their own jobs to do. We needed to heat the cabin on cool evenings. Dad replaced the oil drum with a Franklin stove, and at that time, it was the twins' responsibility to keep it supplied with firewood. Near the house, there were plenty of dead limbs on the ground for them to gather.

Dad put up a sawbuck to hold logs for cutting. The twins learned quickly how to use a bowsaw efficiently, not pushing down, just moving the blade back and forth and letting the saw do the work.

Lanny acted as Dad's step-and-fetch-it person. He kept track of all the tools, held things, handed things, and listened affably while Dad tried to solve the frequent problems.

Dawn helped me inside our unfinished structure. Household tasks always took longer than in more civilized surroundings with modern conveniences. But the work was the same — help with the cooking, dry the dishes, sweep the floor, and take out the trash.

Both Lanny and Dawn were faithful helpers on the mornings before Dad went to town. But the afternoons were theirs for play. Leftover log ends worked just as well on the twins' construction projects as they did on Dad's. They soon created a cosmopolis of forts, houses, and garages; city streets and rural highways carried big dump trucks and tiny matchbox cars. Their efforts tamed the wilderness in an ever-widening circle in our yard.

On some days, the children transported each other around our paths in a red wagon. They kept track of whose turn it was to pull or ride with a precision that amazed me, and they rode the tire swing strung between two birch trees to heights that alarmed me.

On nice days, they went off with a picnic lunch to a bluff overlooking the highway and the valley beyond. Feeling independent, they sat by themselves on a log in the summer sun. As they grew older, they did this in winter, too, whenever they needed to escape from the cabin after days of sub-zero weather.

Lanny blazed new paths through the woods around the house, preparing himself for later years when he would make snowmobile trails for a trapline.

Dawn cared for our pets, loving it when our dog pro-duced a litter. She looked forward to the day when we would have farm ani-mals, and maybe a horse.

We had no TV, of course, but a battery-operated record player entertained them when it rained. Lanny read books about Tarzan and Jane, and Dawn enjoyed stories about the little house on the prairie. Then they fancied the characters from these books in their own play. Their activities were limited only by their imaginations.

I sometimes felt like a kid myself, playing house in our cabin in the woods. Kids live in a private world, filled with opti-mism for the future. In those days, I think both Dad and I were kids in that way, too.

We were free as could be out there. But it was up to all of us to handle our new-found independence. We would be accountable, if only to ourselves, if we succeeded or did not suc-ceed as homesteaders.

Moss &
a Roof

▼▼▼▼▼▼▼▼▼▼▼▼▼▼▼▼▼▼▼▼▼▼▼▼▼▼▼▼▼▼▼▼▼▼▼▼▼▼▼

A s August made its way toward September, the days grew shorter and the nights grew chillier. The fall rains would soon begin.

Dad took a week's vacation and finished the roof. Lanny, Dawn and I set to work to seal or "chink" the cabin walls with moss.

The moss was easy to get. It grew in a thick carpet in the spruce grove up the hill. Each morning, we trudged to the grove and spread canvas tarps under the trees. We pulled up fists full of the green stuff and threw it onto tarps. When it was piled high, we gathered up the tarps, slung them over our shoulders like Santa sacks, and "ho, ho, ho'ed" our way to the yard. There, we spread it all out to dry.

A couple of sunny days was all it took to make the moss dry and pliable enough to fill the cracks in the walls.

Chinking was my job. Working a few feet at a time, I stuffed as much moss as I could into the spaces between the logs. Then, with a table knife, I crammed the moss in as tight as it would go. The result was quite pretty; the house looked like it was dressed up for Christmas.

Of course, that pretty green insulation would dry and shrink as time went by, and fingers of cold would find their way through. But several bags of seasoned moss held in reserve would plug up the holes.

Later, Dad and I would chink the outside walls with a mixture of tar and sawdust, and eventually, smooth white plaster would cover the moss inside.

▼▼▼

The cabin measured 16-by-24 feet, and a porch stretched across the front of it. From the porch, we entered the main room through a door made of double-thick rough lumber, held

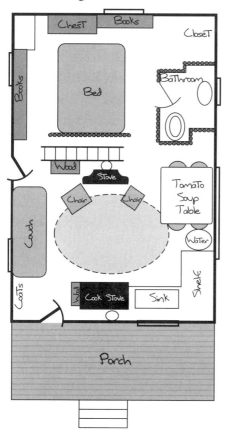

together with a "Z"-shaped brace like an old barn door. A sliding wooden latch with a peg handle closed it snug and tight.

Directly inside the door were the wooden pegs where we hung our coats. Then came the living room area — under the window sat the wobbly couch we purchased third- or fourth-hand. Dad replaced the legs with stubby log ends left over from building, and I planned to make a ruffled slipcover to hide them from sight.

Eventually, we would build a room off the side door, and, just outside, add a patio, barns and sheds.

Across from the door, a spruce ladder angled upstairs through a sliding trapdoor. Lanny and Dawn had bedrooms up under the eaves.

Downstairs, a partial wall of thin spruce poles separated the front and back of the house. They were spaced far enough apart for heat to flow between them, and hopefully, close enough together to provide privacy. Our bedroom was in the back, along with a bathroom of sorts — that is, it looked like a bathroom anywhere, but there were no faucets or pipes.

Back in the front room, The Tomato Soup Table sat with four brand-new chairs under a broad window looking out over the woods and valley. It was just like we'd talked about that first day, a year ago, sitting against the log.

The kitchen, equipped with a skeleton of a sink, was in the front corner of the cabin. Next to the sink was a wood-burning cookstove. And right square in the middle of the house was the black Franklin stove. The doors opened in front so we could sit and look at the fire. For seating, we made do with lawn chairs brought in for the winter until Dad had time to do some furniture building.

By then, the floors were varnished. On order from Sears were braided rugs for the living room, and frilly pink and blue plaid accessories for the twins' rooms upstairs. Yet to come were mellow pine cabinets, ruffled window curtains, and hanging plants for the rest of the house.

And finally, we notified the State of Alaska Correspondence School program of our need for two sets of school lessons.

We were ready to settle in.

Bringing Home the Goods

▼▼▼▼▼▼▼▼▼▼▼▼▼▼▼▼▼▼▼▼▼▼▼▼▼▼▼▼▼▼▼▼▼▼▼

One night, I waited excitedly for Dad to travel from Fairbanks with the box trailer filled with our belongings. It would be so nice to have them around the house! All the little things that make a house a home — boxes of books, curtains from my mother, the good dishes, and all our winter clothes — were waiting in town to come to a suitable home.

The plan was that Dad would pick up the trailer after work at 11 p.m. and drive home. At 1 a.m., I heard the truck door close at the foot of the hill. It seemed to take a long time for Dad to reach the house.

I grinned happily as he walked in the door, but his expression took the smile from my face.

"What's the matter?" I asked.

"Well," he answered, "when I turned up the driveway I thought I heard a thump from behind. I got out of the truck and went to look. I saw a box on the ground, fallen out of the trailer. The back door must have come off."

"But don't worry," he consoled me, "I looked around pretty good with a flashlight, and I think the only thing broken was one of your egg cups."

"Oh, my gosh!" I said. "The dishes were packed in the *middle* of the trailer! Where's all the other stuff?"

We had pulled that trailer all the way across the country without any problems; Dad had packed it up tight. Over the summer, I had taken a few things out, but I thought I'd closed it up again good.

There was nothing Dad could do but go scouting.

As Dad told it, there was fresh snow on the road and his were the only tire tracks. He retraced his journey, stopping every so often to pick up our possessions which were easily seen in the light of the headlamps. It seemed to him he'd be all night on this recovery trip.

But after about 20 miles, he met another pickup coming toward him. Dad stopped, blinked his lights, and the other truck pulled next to him.

"Have you happened to see any household goods along the road on your way out?" he asked.

"Have we! The first thing we found was a trailer door about 25 miles back. Since then, we've picked up boxes, toys, a typewriter, more boxes, coat hangers, and even some photographs. Are they yours?"

Sure enough, the back of their pickup was loaded with our stuff. They followed Dad home to our cabin for coffee.

By then, it was 3:30 in the morning, but nobody cared. Our benefactors were on a hunting trip, and right then, time meant nothing to us — we had our belongings!

We laughed and joked at the table, and pretty soon Lanny and Dawn came down the ladder to see what was going on.

"That's them!" cried one of the hunters. "That's the kids in the photographs." In case they'd had any doubts, they knew then that all those things were really ours.

All's well that ends well. In due time, everything was brought into the house and put away. Surrounded by our belongings, we were finally home.

The Cookstove: Heart of the Homestead

vvvvvvvvvvvvvvvvvvvvvvvvvvvvvvvvvvvvvvvvvvvvvvv

"**L**et's make a pot of coffee," I said as we stood admiring our brand new Sears wood range.

Back when Dad laid the log rounds for the cabin, this heavy iron cookstove was already in place on the subfloor, protected from the elements by a heavy tarp. Before we could cook with it, we had to put on the roof, build the stone chimney, and install the stovepipe.

I couldn't wait to start using it. I could just see myself capably cooking in my old-fashioned but efficient kitchen, serving delectable homestead meals.

We loaded the range with wood, lit the fire, and put the coffee pot on.

Mmm, wouldn't that taste good?

The coffee started to perk, one bubble, then another, then stopped. We looked in the firebox. The wood had all burned up!

Well, start another fire and get it going again.

However, by the time the new fire was burning, the iron stove top had cooled to lukewarm and had to be heated up again.

But, within an hour, we were pouring steaming cups of black brew which we swore was the best we had ever tasted.

That was the beginning of my acquaintance with the wood cookstove. It was quite a while before we got to know each other well.

One thing the stove demanded was plenty of dry spruce kindling to get it going. Then it had to be fed chunks of birch wood — many small pieces to boil coffee, a few large pieces to simmer a pot roast. Of course, I had to remember to keep feeding it; Dad often went to work after gobbling down a meal that hadn't been ready until 10 minutes before he had to leave.

But soon I got used to the stove. I found that the cook top radiated various degrees of heat when I moved the pots closer to, or farther from, the fire box.

Why, it was just like turning switches on my old electric!

The two warming ovens on top were true to their names and a blessing to me when I was cooking dinner. I could never get the meat and vegetables done at the same time. But by popping dishes into the warming ovens, I still served the whole meal at once, piping hot.

I was beginning to feel quite confident with my new stove. After all, we'd been baking bread and cookies over an oil drum all summer; I should be able to bake anything in this new oven.

But baking cakes and having them come out right was a real contest. The oven had a little thermometer that I could make say "350 degrees," but I couldn't get it to stay there during the baking. A pan of cake batter, which I had lovingly mixed by hand, would be set inside just at the right temperature and would come out a flat, gooey dough or a hard, black brick depending on how much wood was in the firebox and which way I moved the oven dampers.

But, with much trial and error, I learned the right combinations. Finally, I was able to produce angel food cakes and even cheese souffles that I was proud to serve.

Life centered around the cookstove. It was lit first thing in the morning and the coffee put on; and it was fed faithfully or no breakfast, lunch, or supper. It heated my iron, and burned the trash. It helped keep the cabin warm.

It heated pans of dishwater and washtubs full of bath water; it dried wet firewood and warmed cold pajamas in its oven. And it called for armload after armload of wood to be brought in by the kids.

But more than that, it set the pace of our days. There was no setting the alarm for the last minute, no grabbing a quick bite to eat, no taking a hasty bath. Old Stove didn't know the meaning of the word "hurry," and, after a while, neither did we. The hustle and bustle went out of our lives, tempered by the iron will of our wood-burning cookstove.

Let There Be Light

▼▼▼▼▼▼▼▼▼▼▼▼▼▼▼▼▼▼▼▼▼▼▼▼▼▼▼▼▼▼▼▼▼▼▼▼▼▼

I t's hard to break the habit of reaching for the lightswitch when entering a dark house. Thus it was when we walked into our cabin at night. I would fumble along the wall looking for a switch — every time — but of course, there was none. The nearest power line was 50 miles away.

Instead, I would have to feel my way over to the metal box hanging on the kitchen cupboard and get out a match.

Then there were a variety of choices.

Next to the cupboard, on The Tomato Soup Table, stood an Aladdin™ lamp. I would remove the shade and chimney, turn the wick up and light it, then replace the chimney and shade. I was careful never to turn it up too high. The flame would flare up and smoke would pour from the chimney covering its innards with hard, black soot. If I turned the wick too low, the light would go out in a minute. This was a lamp that needed someone to sit by it, tenderly adjusting its wick up and down according to its whims.

On the walls were two gaslights with round globes and efficient silk-spun mantles that could put forth the brilliance of 60-watt light bulbs. Copper tubing carried the propane to them from tanks outside in the yard. They were simple to light; just turn a handle, listen for the gas to hiss, and put the lighted match close to the mantle. But, oh, not too close! It was so easy to puncture the fragile mantle, and then that lamp would smoke up, too.

The most manageable lamps were the kerosenes with cloth wicks that were scattered throughout the rest of the house. They lit without trouble and behaved themselves. But they only illuminated dimly a small space around them.

The lamps did a passable job. The children did their schoolwork under the light of the Aladdin™ lamp. The gaslights gave general illumination and, if we huddled up close, we could read by the kerosene lamps.

As fall drew into winter, the lights were lit earlier and earlier in the afternoon. Pretty soon we needed morning lights, too. When December came, they were on all day.

By the time the long nights of winter were over, we were all pretty frustrated with nebulous lighting. Though it was good enough for general kitchen work, I had to feel with my fingers to tell if the dishes were really clean. I could knit and sew, but threading a needle could be baffling. Paperback books with small print were put away until spring, and if the kids dropped something in a dark corner, it stayed there for the duration; there was no way to find it. They had treasure hunts for tinker toys along about April.

But on the other hand, late on winter evenings, as I waited for Dad to come home, our lackluster lights fostered a tranquillity that no electric bulb could imitate. The lamps in the windows waited with their warm glow to welcome him as he walked up the hill. When he came in, we would sit by the stove and have a cup of tea. Soon the flicker of the flames would cast their spell and make our eyelids droop. Gentle shadows and intermittent crackling from the stove would surround us, lulling us into repose.

Then, we would blow out the lights, one by one, and go to bed.

The Bucket Chores

Nothing was automatic on our homestead. We heated with wood stoves. We worked and studied under lamplight. There were no faucets on our sinks; we poured water into them from jugs and pitchers. Six-gallon buckets stood underneath the sinks, and whatever went into the sinks drained into the buckets.

In the bathroom, there was an up-to-date, ventilated, oval-shaped homestead toilet that contained a large galvanized bucket. Standing around outside the house were other buckets: water buckets, snow buckets and ash buckets.

It was my responsibility each day to take care of the bucket chores.

The bucket under the kitchen sink was my nemesis. No matter how I tried to conserve water while washing dishes, nor how often I peeked into the lower cupboard to check on the bucket, it was invariably full to the brim. Tugging, heaving, balancing, and wiping up spills, I transported it to the stoop outside the back door.

Next to empty was the galvanized biffy bucket from the bathroom. Wearing heavy gloves, I toted the bucket down the path to our log outhouse. (This was a comfortable building with windows and a good view we often used on nice days.) I dumped the bucket, rinsed it with soapy dishwater, and carried it to the slop-water dumping spot at the edge of the woods. Unpleasant as this job was, it was better than hustling down the trail every few hours day and night, in bad weather, to use the outhouse.

These were not my only bucket chores.

In winter, we kept a 30-gallon container of snow in the house to melt for wash and utility water. It was my job to gather the snow. Also, the wood ashes needed to be cleaned from the stoves to keep the fires burning well. Each day, I emptied the ashes into a large container outdoors; they would be used to sprinkle the driveway when the hill was icy.

On some days, these chores did not go smoothly. The bucket under the sink was known to overflow; this meant I had to empty the lower cupboard of its contents, mop up the water, wipe out the cupboard, and dry it out. (This did not happen often after the first experience.) Also, the unexpected arrival of company just at the moment I carried the buckets to the outhouse created a social situation I would hesitate to ask Emily Post about!

All in all, I didn't mind the bucket chores. They got me outside for a few minutes each day, especially on days I might never have had a breath of fresh air. These were the final tasks of my daily housekeeping, and I had a sense of order and accomplishment when they were done.

But, I thought, if ever again I lived in a house with faucets and pipes and everything automatic, I would look back on these days, and I would not miss my bucket chores!

A Homestead Shower

▼▲▼▲▼▲▼▲▼▲▼▲▼▲▼▲▼▲▼▲▼▲▼▲▼▲▼▲▼▲▼▲▼▲▼▲▼

N ot long after we moved into our cabin, I had a long-ing for a luxurious, hot bath. I kept a bottle of sweet-smelling bath oil in the cabinet, just waiting to be used.

By then we had a tub — galvanized, three feet in diameter, with handles. We had bought this for bathing because it filled up with just a few buckets of water. For eight-year-olds, the tub's size was okay; but for grown-ups, it was not very practical.

Nevertheless, one day when the family was away, I heated kettles on the cookstove and filled the tub with water and several doses of bubble bath oil and got in. Scrunching down and squeezing in, I submerged underneath the bubbles.

Ahhhh, heavenly bliss!

But, sad to say, in a little while the water cooled down, and the cabin did too; the fire in the cookstove had burned out. Besides that, my muscles had taken a set. Trying to get out, I realized I was stuck in my galvanized tub. Should I try to wrench myself out? Or should I wait for Dad to get back? What if company came in the meantime? I was starting to shiver! Finally, with the greatest effort and wrenching my shoulder,

I extricated myself. I ached all the next week. That was the end of the three-foot tub.

After that, we bought a full-sized oblong homesteaders' tub, roomy enough for a fine bubble bath. It also held a full day's supply of water. With four people to bathe each week, we soon found ourselves in short supply. Also, someone had to empty out those gallons and gallons of water after the bath. That took many trips with the bucket. It turned out not worth the effort to use, and the tub hung outside the back door and got dusty.

The coin-operated showers at the Laundromat in town were our last resort. They were very distasteful to us. On one hot June day, the coin box stopped working in the middle of a shower, and the water turned off before the soap was rinsed off.

That was it! Somehow, some way, we had to find a way to take a bath at home.

In a catalog, we found a shower stall that would just fit in the corner of the bathroom if we sacrificed half a closet behind it. A plastic water tank from a motor home catalog would fit snugly up under the eaves. We sent for them both, and Dad installed the shower and hooked it to the tank upstairs. We pumped water up with our battery pump and waited for the water to spray from the shower head. A little trickle came out and dribbled down the wall — not enough pressure.

Undaunted, we tried another route. Bypassing the shower head with the hose from our hot water bottle, we strung it into a homemade shower head — a peanut can with holes punched into the bottom. The shower worked something like a sprinkling can, but it did the job. The water then drained into a funnel which went through a hole in the floor and into the ground underneath the house.

This shower was a success. It kept us clean for many years. Best of all, it took only one six-gallon bucket full of water. We had solved our bath problem. And I didn't even long for a bubble bath anymore.

The Radio –
Our Home Companion

▼▼▼▼▼▼▼▼▼▼▼▼▼▼▼▼▼▼▼▼▼▼▼▼▼▼▼▼▼▼▼▼▼▼▼▼

One of our most important possessions on the homestead was our battery-powered radio. It played a daily part in our lives; it was our communication with the world.

It kept us up on what was going on around us, and kept us aware that even though we saw no one outside of our family for days and sometimes weeks on end, there were other people out there.

Besides listening to the news programs and weather reports, we tuned in to *Tundra Topics*, a message service that one of the stations aired every night at 9:20. When the theme song of *Mush, You Huskies* came on, all of us in the house stopped what we were doing and turned our ears to the radio. Messages from folks in town were phoned into the station and sent to people all over the Interior this way.

Some were brief and concise: "To George, near Livengood, from Jackovich Tractor and Equipment Co. The part for your generator is in."

Some were friendly messages: "To the Merriweathers on the Elliott from the Conroys in Fairbanks. Coming to visit on Saturday; will bring salad and dessert."

Some of the messages that came over the air were quite exciting: "To my husband at Rampart from Louise at Tanana Hospital. I had a baby boy last night — 7 pounds, 3 ounces. Will fly home on Saturday."

Others were somber: "To John Jones somewhere out of Fairbanks from Aunt Mary in Minneapolis. Your mother has passed away; please call home."

We listened for messages for us. We might be having visitors, too, or something we ordered might have come in. And we kept a wary ear open for the other kind of message.

Every day at news time and in the evening, we listened to our radio. As the voices from the other end droned on or pattered away, we listened solemnly or sang along.

The radio had an odd control over our lives. I remember listening late one Christmas night as I waited for Dad to come home. Lovely carols were playing. The station had outdone itself in putting us all in the Christmas spirit that season, and I was enjoying it up to the end.

At midnight, a short commercial came on. After that, I knew Christmas was over when *Jeremiah Was A Bullfrog* blared out of the speaker. That would be all the *Joy to the World* we would hear until next year.

At the New Year, we used the radio to count down the last few seconds of the old year so we'd know when to celebrate.

"Five seconds, four seconds, three, two, one...HAPPY NEW YEAR!" shouted the announcer on KFAR.

Hugs and kisses followed, and we waited for *Auld Lang Syne*. But that station didn't play it; they had news instead. So we turned to KFRB.

"Just a couple more minutes till midnight!" proclaimed the announcer there.

We got to celebrate all over again. Who knew which station was on the right time? In Alaska in those days, each station kept its own time.

The announcers we heard every day turned into acquaintances over the years. I would picture each one — tall and young, or old and squat, according to his voice. I'd "see" their faces before me, some rugged and strong, others clean-cut and sensitive. What a shock it was to see the same announcers on TV at someone's house in town, and have them look completely different!

But it really didn't matter. Our radio took on a personality of its own as time went by. It brought us good news and bad, and made us happy and sad. Like a good friend, it was always there.

It was indispensable.

AROUND THE FARM

Proving Up

▼▼▼▼▼▼▼▼▼▼▼▼▼▼▼▼▼▼▼▼▼▼▼▼▼▼▼▼▼▼▼▼▼▼▼▼

In order to gain title to a homestead in Alaska, the government set forth several conditions.

First, of course, was to find a suitable site. In our case, the area was unsurveyed land. In order to file for a homestead, Dad had to locate the corners of the property. The closest reference point was a bridge over the river about five miles down the road. To establish the first corner, Dad made careful measurements using the odometer on our truck, and posted a sign on a large birch tree. Then he plotted the rest of the 160-acres on paper, and officially filed with the Bureau of Land Management (BLM). The next summer, he and Lanny made a physical survey using a hand-held prismatic compass and a 100-foot steel tape.

Second was a period of residency — we had to live on the land for three to five years.

And finally, we had to clear and plant 10-acres of land in two years with the reasonable expectation of a crop.

Meeting these conditions was called "proving up."

There was no fooling around with these requirements. The BLM made sure that a family had lived on their land for an exact number of days. Their investigators measured the cleared acres and looked over the crop — or, if it hadn't grown up yet, dug down into the soil to find the seed.

▼▼▼

The summer after we moved into our cabin, we made arrangements to have our 10-acres cleared. Dad chose a spot on one end of the homestead, about a quarter mile from the house. Our friend, Fred, brought out his DC-6 Cat bulldozer on a big truck, and stayed on our couch for the duration of the job.

First, Fred and Dad paced off the right amount of land in the woods. Then Fred and his "Cat" started knocking over spruce and birch trees. For three days he pushed and scraped, shoving timber and root masses into four berm piles that reached nearly the length of the clearing.

I hated to see even this small portion of our beautiful forest destroyed and have to look at the ugly gash left behind. But Dad focussed only on the final result; he was already figuring how many bags of fertilizer and seed we would need.

After Fred left, the clearing was still covered with large pieces of roots, rocks, and other things that had to be moved by hand. Dad, Lanny and Dawn spent days on end dragging and hauling debris to the berm piles. This was probably the most detested job that the twins and all homestead children ever had to do.

Over the next few weeks, Dad plowed and used the disk harrow to break up and level the plowed ground. He attached it to the tractor we had bought in the spring.

Then, as I drove the tractor, Dad stood in the wagon behind me, throwing out fertilizer in wide arcs with a shovel.

When that was finished, we started the seeding. This was done by hand and it took several days. Both of us carried bags of brome grass seed over our shoulders, as we walked up and down and back and forth across the clearing, broadcasting handfuls of seed to each side.

Looking ahead, I envisioned lush, green fields of hay. But only scattered shoots of grass showed themselves that summer. Raw land, late planting, and bad weather took their tolls. Legally, however, we had met the requirements on time.

In the wintertime, Dad cut up the wood we had moved to the scraggly edges of the berm piles. When spring came, we saw shoots of raspberries protruding from the middle of the berms, and by the second year, we had a fine crop of wild berries.

Through the following years, we planted the clearing again and again, experimenting with various grasses and grains. Each year, the fields grew better and provided more feed for our animals. In the lower field, we planted potatoes, and they grew to great size.

In due time, the cabin and the clearing were inspected by the federal surveyors. They made official measurements of the homestead, barely straying from Dad's and Lanny's lines. The BLM man wrote that we had a fine home, and that our hayfields, buckwheat plots, and potato patch (not to mention the wild raspberry crop), had completely fulfilled the home-steading requirements.

We had proven up!

The Mighty M

If there was one thing that could have made or broken our homesteading success in Alaska, it was our Model M International farm tractor. Dad called it the "Mighty M."

Thirty years old, but powerful as 40 horses, it had no frills whatsoever. The seat was made of hard steel. The steering wheel required all my strength to turn. And, when its unreliable battery didn't work, Dad had to use an old-fashioned hand crank to start it up.

But with attachments, that tractor could do anything — pull stumps, saw wood and plow snow. Dad also used it to cultivate and mow the fields, and along with an old-time dump rake (circa 1935), he made neat piles of brome grass and hay.

After that, Dad and Lanny worked together to bring in the crop. Dad used a pitchfork to lift huge bunches of hay onto a big wagon. And Lanny stood on top and trampled it down the old-fashioned way to make room for more. Our son must be one of a very few of his generation in Alaska who learned how to build a load of hay on a wagon properly.

When it was time for the last load of the season to be brought in, we'd invite our friends out for a hayride. Dad drove as we chugged around our 10-acre clearing, singing and laughing. Then we'd come back to the house for a harvest potluck dinner.

▼▼▼

After a few years, Dad bought a new attachment for the Mighty M — a front loader with hydraulic arms that lifted and carried things from one place to another. In the springtime, the loader bucket dug into our gravel pit with its teeth and scraped up fill. Then it dropped the load onto our muddy driveway.

That front loader was a real work saver, and probably a lifesaver, too. Before we had it, we used an ancient iron scoop called a slip-scraper to dig gravel. It had two long wooden handles on its back, and was connected to the tractor with a chain. Dad, the scoop operator, put all his weight on the handles to make the scoop dig in. As the tractor operator, I was supposed to drag the scoop very slowly along the ground. But no matter how gently I eased up on the clutch pedal, the tractor took off with a jerk, and Dad would flip over the top of the scoop hollering STOP!

On one job, Dad asked Lanny to operate the tractor. They needed to move our heavy log outhouse over a new hole. With all the ropes and pulleys set, Dad told Lanny to ease up on the clutch — gradually. But Lanny didn't have any better coordination than I did; the outhouse literally flew several feet through the air.

Amazingly, it landed squarely on top of the new hole!

Dad wasn't always so lucky with the tractor. One winter morning, when he started it up, he found the battery dead. So he put the crank in place and turned it. The motor coughed, then died; the heavy crank reversed and slammed back against his arm, and telltale black lines near his wrist showed two cracked bones. We splinted his arm and wrapped it in a bandage. He split our kindling one-handed that day before he drove to work.

On another occasion, when the ground in the clearing looked dry and firm, Dad decided to get a little ahead of the game and start plowing in May. But the dry surface of the soil was deceiving, and the tractor's big wheels sank up to the axles in mud. There was nothing to do but leave the tractor right where it was and walk home.

After 10 days of sunshine, Dad went to the field and tried again. From the house I heard the "POP, POP" of the engine and a steady hum. I knew he had backed out of the hole, and I could picture him sitting on the unyielding seat — his steel throne — king of all he surveyed, driving around the clearing and singing an old-time song.

The Mighty M was back in business.

The Garden

▼▼

I n March of each year, though several feet of snow usually covered the ground, we began to think about spring. We put on our list of things to do in Fairbanks: "Buy seeds." On town day, we planned extra time at the supermarket; it had the most complete seed counter of all the stores.

The seed rack was the first stop we would make with our shopping cart. We studied the packages carefully. There was little debate on what to plant in the vegetable garden: root crops; cole crops like cabbage; and peas, beans, and squash. One year, Lanny and Dawn put packages with pictures of long ears of corn into the basket. We switched those to the shorter-eared Yukon type. In Interior Alaska, it is important to buy varieties that mature in the shortest number of days.

Flowers were not as easy to choose. The pictures on the seed packets were all so pretty. My imagination soared as I dreamed of exotic blossoms lining our walks and driveway. But soon, Dad would walk off impatiently to the hardware department, followed shortly by the twins. So I would hastily pick up the old standbys: marigolds, calendulas, and petunias. Grabbing a bag of potting soil, our garden was inaugurated.

At home, I filled flats with potting soil and planted the seeds that needed an early start. Some were so tiny, I needed my glasses to see that I didn't plant more than one to a spot. It seemed unbelievable that these would grow into giant cabbages, bushy broccoli or cascading petunias.

Soon, my tidy little flats of vegetables and flowers grew into thick jungles. Scrawny seedlings tangled together with new leaves reaching for the light. They had to be transplanted, of course, into many flats.

At that time of year, flats took up every inch of shelf and table space by the windows inside the cabin. We worked and ate around them, waiting for the ground outside to get warm and dry so the garden could be tilled.

In early June, the garden beds were ready — tilled fine and mixed with manure. We set out the plants according to the directions on the seed packets. Three to four feet apart for the cabbages seemed like quite a distance for our seedlings; they looked lonely in their allotted spaces. And those little flower starts could never cover the ground with blazing color like the seed package showed, it seemed.

Dawn and I sowed seeds for lettuce, carrots, peas, and radishes. Crawling around on our hands and knees, we dropped them one or two inches apart, and covered them with a dusting of soil.

Dad and Lanny planted a sack full of potatoes over in the clearing, each with a little dab of manure.

Finally, the time came to stand back, and have faith that these black plots of soil would, with the sun and the rain, grow into luxuriant gardens. They would become vegetables to feed our family for the winter, and flowers to pretty up our home-stead for the summer.

Around the farm

By July, we were eating garden-fresh salad.

The spotty little garden that had looked so forlorn had turned into lush green rows. Holding the seed packets that we had planted such a short time ago, I marveled that I could hold in my hand the beginnings of this garden that spread before me.

By August, we were eating regularly from the garden, and the chickens were inundated with surplus greens to munch. In early September, when the air was golden with the turning birch leaves, we harvested the rest.

Baskets of root crops and cabbages were stored away in cool corners of the cabin. Feed bags of potatoes were stuffed into the back of the closet and layered with blankets to keep heat away. Orange and green squashes sat on shelves among vases of marigolds and calendulas.

We prided ourselves on what we called "Homestead Dinners." With everything on the table coming from our own land in such bounty, we invited company from town to share these meals with us. I remember one friend patting his tummy after a dinner of fried chicken, mashed potatoes, corn on the cob, and green salad. He pushed back from The Tomato Soup Table and said, "People in town who live in big, modern houses with all the facilities and everything handy feel so sorry for you."

"Oh," they say, "how you must suffer way out here at the ragged edge of the wilderness!"

I thought of our comfortable house bulging with produce as I edged up to the warm Franklin stove and looked at the contented faces all around. Outside the window, a huge harvest moon rose over the valley.

Oh, my yes, I thought. *How we suffer!*

Chickens
& Geese

▼▼

One of our objectives was to create a little farm where we would raise animals, feel self-sufficient, and teach our children values they might not learn in the city.

So one June day, we bought a brood of 50 Rhode Island Red chickens, just one day old. They had been hatched Outside (in the Lower 48), flown to Fairbanks, and delivered to our local feed store. They sat huddled in a corner of their box, tiny as babies' fists, even with the yellow fuzz that covered them. When we picked them up, they chirped in high-pitched complaint.

We held the box across our laps in the pickup for the long drive home. At every bump, the chicks peeped frightfully; they seemed such fragile little things.

That first night, we kept them in the house. The next day, Dad built them temporary living quarters — an insulated box with an attached covered wire pen. It was 90 degrees outside, but we still put a jar of hot water wrapped with a towel in the box so they wouldn't get chilled. Even so, they crowded together in one end, and several of the weaker ones died the first few days.

The rest, however, grew rapidly. They emptied the mash from their feeding trough five times a day and started feathering out. Bold and active, they soon outgrew their pen and needed additional space.

Dad built them a log chicken house, and by mid-July, the chicks were nestled safely inside.

▼▼▼

One day, when we went to the feed store to pick up supplies, we were entranced by other fuzzy creatures peeping about in their cages. Especially cute were the little baby geese with their elongated necks and sharp eyes.

We bought half a dozen. We knew that the goslings would quickly grow bigger than the chicks and would beat on them if we kept them together. So, the geese were given a little pen of their own. It wasn't long before we let them out to exercise. Along they would go in a line, following the person who had opened the door for them — bonding with us as they would with their mother, I suppose.

As the geese grew, they demanded the freedom of the yard. They waddled about, investigating everything and everybody, making funny little honking sounds and tripping over every stick and fallen leaf in their way.

As their feathers grew, they thought they should be able to fly. Several times a day they practiced, using the upper driveway as a runway. En masse like a squadron, they ran along on floppy feet, flapping their wings. But they never could get their bottoms off the ground; they were too heavy from a diet of cracked corn.

Their favorite sport was swimming in our old oblong homesteader's bathtub. They'd climb up the ramp Dad built for them and tumble headfirst into the tub, one after the other. Then, all chaos would break loose as they pushed, shoved, and honked at each other, splashing water on the ground.

As they matured, they ventured from the boundary of the yard toward the road at the foot of the hill. If we heard a car tooting its horn we knew why — and one of us would go fetch the geese, herding them by holding a long pole over their backs.

Soon, we realized, it was time to start butchering them. After finishing off the first four and standing knee deep in feathers, we decided we'd had enough of that. We would keep the two remaining birds for pets.

That goose and gander made the most of their pet status on the homestead. They intimidated the dogs and filched their food. As we sat outside, the white gander nipped at our chair legs, then at our pant legs, and then at our legs. Then, he'd get hauled by the neck, his webbed feet dragging, and get tossed into the goose pond. That would make him forget his mischief, and soon, he'd be waddling along with his mate, honking over her shoulder, making the rounds of the yard.

Even in their clumsiness, their snow-white bodies and tall stature seem to give an air of elegance around the place.

▼▼▼

Meanwhile, back at the henhouse, the chickens kept growing. In a couple of months they were overcrowded again, so we started butchering them, too.

First thing in the morning, I heated several kettles of water on the stove. Dad and Lanny headed for the chicken yard with an axe and a bucket and rounded up the first roosters. Dawn and I, both chicken-hearted, stayed inside with the radio on. Afterwards, Lanny and Dawn plucked feathers; Dad and I dressed out the birds.

Every Sunday we ate a chicken, and when company came, we ate two chickens. We never tired of it; that fresh poultry tasted better than any we had ever bought in a store.

By then, our chicken flock was just about the right size — enough hens for laying, and a big red rooster named "Brewster" to keep them happy.

Brewster had established himself at the top of the pecking order. He also considered himself a step above nine-year-old Lanny, whose job it was to feed the flock. Every day, the rooster stalked Lanny and, when the chance came, hurled himself at the boy with beak biting and spurs digging. Lanny was getting scared to go into the henhouse.

"Show him who's boss," said Dad. "That rooster will never stop attacking you until you do."

The next morning Lanny, in his own way, did just that. When Brewster rushed him, Lanny picked up the bird and held him tight against his coat. He whirled around — and around and around — until both of them were dizzy. Then he threw Brewster into a corner and walked out. Brewster had the last word; he cock-a-doodle-doo'ed from the corner.

But Brewster never bothered Lanny again.

▼▼▼

Eagerly, we awaited the first egg. Whenever a hen cackled, one of us went to see if she had laid one. But it was always a false alarm. Finally one day, Lanny brought in the prize — a great big double yolker — and had the honor of eating it for breakfast.

Those first fresh eggs were a new treat for all of us. The dark yellow yolks stood up high and the whites did not spread all over the pan. They tasted so good, that we were known to have fried eggs for breakfast, egg salad sandwiches for lunch, and omelets for supper. Every day, it seemed, there would be more eggs than the day before. Lanny went out periodically to collect them and put them in the pocket of his parka. When he came in, he'd pull them out, one by one, while he counted. I remember one day when he counted, "one, two, three, four." Then an anguished expression came over his face. I couldn't help laugh as he pulled a gooey, broken egg from his pocket.

We kept our eggs in a bowl, but when the hens started laying steadily, it overflowed.

So Dad sold eggs at work.

He had regular customers who would buy a dozen on specified days of the week. So starved for fresh eggs were these Alaskans, that Dad had to hide the carton until that day's buyer came to pick up his order — or they would be demanded by other egg lovers.

▼▼▼

The geese were not economically productive, except for a huge egg once in a while that would feed two people, and the chickens barely paid for their keep, even with our egg sales. But they redeemed themselves by providing us with good food and the satisfaction of raising them.

And, after many years, everyone in our family still appreciates a good fresh egg.

Goats

N ow that we had settled down to be farmers, it was time, we thought, to get a cow.

Dad went to our feed man for advice.

"You don't want a cow, sir," he was told. "Cows give way too much milk for a family your size, and they don't get along well in this climate. What you need is a goat!"

And he had goats for sale.

So we bought Betty, a black Toggenburg with a homely white face. Her flat eyes mirrored a good many years of living. Her horns were crumpled and scarred. We brought her home with her two day-old baby kids, and moved them all into a shed attached to the chicken house while Dad built a barn. But the rainy season set in, and one little goat got chilled and died. Frantically, we moved the other baby, Bonnie, in the house into a little pen in the corner, until the barn was finished. We fed her with a bottle four times a day and changed her hay at least that often. She was a good little kid; she slept all night and didn't stir until we did in the morning.

By then, the barn was Dad's first priority, and he got it done in jig time. Mother and daughter were soon moved in and settled down.

We stocked up on goat chow and chicken feed, turned the chicken house into a feed house, and transferred the chickens to one side of the new barn. Dad set up our old oil-drum stove in the middle of the barn to use when the temperature went below zero.

Now our little farm was ready for year-round residency.

Betty provided all the fresh milk we needed, with some left over. With this, I made a creamy cheese that spread on bread like butter and was twice as good. Dad learned how to make hard cheese.

Betty was milked twice a day — at noon just before Dad went to work, and a little after midnight when he got home.

It was important, as all farmers know, that she be milked on time. But sometimes Dad was late coming home from work, and I'd have to do it. I was not very adept at the task; I'd wait until the very last minute that my conscience would allow.

Finally, I'd get out of bed, pull warm clothes over my pajamas, light the lantern, and go out to the barn. I'd give Betty her grain, sit down on the milking stand, and start in. Tiny trickles of milk would squirt into the bucket as I squeezed and pulled her teats.

Squeeze, pull, squeeze, pull — Betty would finish her grain and wait calmly.

Squeeze, pull — my fingers would start to ache.

Patient Betty would turn her head around hopefully, then gently rub her old horns up and down my back.

A half-hour later the job was done, and I'd go back to the house to strain the milk. More often than not, Dad would come up the drive at that time — too late, too soon. I was happy when the children got old enough to do the milking, morning and evening.

In nice weather, we let Betty and Bonnie out to browse. They liked to nibble young birch trees, but would try anything tender and green; we enclosed the garden with a four-foot fence.

The goats were the nicest animals we had on the homestead. Exceptionally friendly, they loved to hang around us in the yard, nuzzling up often to get their ears scratched.

They also got into things. A bowl of potato chips set out for a picnic was fair game to them. So was anything left on the ground — like the directions on how to put together the 250 piece front-loader attachment for our tractor.

But they were worth the trouble. Not only for the fun they provided and the affection they gave, but economically, too.

We eventually bought a billy goat, so Betty had a number of offspring that later brought us a good price. Also, this meant that we had a steady supply of milk. Considering the high price of milk in stores, the goats paid for themselves very well.

Betty became a grandmother and a great-grandmother, and she tended (and nursed!) her progeny along with their mothers. As grand matriarch, she watched the young kids gambol and frolic with pleasure. Her white face, which we had once thought to be so homely, turned out to be beautiful after all.

Gathering Firewood

On our homestead, we heated the cabin with a Franklin fireplace. Every hour or so we had to feed it with chunks of wood. In the living room, our wood rack extended from the floor to the ceiling. It was kept full according to how low the thermometer went outside. The kindling box by the cookstove filled and emptied at the same ratio.

Every two weeks in wintertime, Dad and Lanny took a day to cut firewood. After breakfast, Dad would ready the chainsaw he'd brought inside the night before to

warm up. After covering the kitchen table with newspapers, he'd snap the cover plate from the saw, dig through its innards, and pick out oily gobs of old birch sawdust. As he finished his coffee, he polished and lubricated each working part of the saw and sharpened each of the chain's 36 teeth with a file.

Scrape, screech, scrape, screech — the sound was like Teacher scratching chalk along the blackboard.

When he was done, father and son bundled themselves into their parkas and boots and went outside. Dad filled the fuel can with a chainsaw mix and Lanny fetched the toboggan and axe. Then the two of them would trudge up the hill to the wood lot.

Pretty soon, I'd hear the steady buzz of the saw and the heavy thump of a birch tree hitting the ground. The engine made short "brr" sounds as the limbs were whisked off and cut up, and longer whining sounds as the trunk was sawed into 18-inch lengths. Lanny's job was to stack the chunks in a pile so they wouldn't get lost in the snow, or, if Dad cut a spruce tree, he used the axe to slice off the short stickers along the trunk. When they'd cut enough trees, they came down to lunch dripping with perspiration despite the 20 or 30 below zero temperatures outside.

After a break, and with dry shirts and full stomachs, they'd go back to fetch the wood and bring it down to the house. Dawn and I often brought the sled along to help. The birch chunks were unbelievably heavy and slippery in snowy, mittened hands. I usually opted for the spruce, which wasn't so unwieldy, especially the dead spruce that Dad cut for kindling.

We piled the wood on the toboggan and sled and slid them downhill — girls on the front and boys behind to pull back on the rope — and then down to the yard for splitting.

Darkness came in early afternoon, but if the moon was shining, we could still see enough in the snowy whiteness to follow the shadow of the toboggan trail down the hill.

But we trod our way carefully.

"Watch it, there's a stick across the trail here."

"Should we try for one more load after this?"

"I'm hungry. What's for supper?" We kept our voices low as we threaded our way alongside the silent woods.

When Dad cut trees, he didn't like to wear cumbersome snowshoes; he wanted to be out of the way when a tree fell, and that would mean undoing laces just before he cut the last few inches of trunk to jump clear. We found that tree trunks have a way of springing backwards sometimes when they fall.

Usually, the snow on the trail stayed packed enough between cuttings to hold us up. But if there had been a heavy snowfall before wood-cutting day, the children and I would have to snowshoe beforehand over the paths and around the trees to be cut. We'd walk up the hill in a line — three pairs of snowshoes making a new trail. Circling the trees, we'd stamp our feet hard like old-time gandy dancers. If the temperature was zero or below, the snow would be hard and firm by the next day.

Dad and Lanny liked low temperatures for splitting the wood — the colder the better. The chunks would crack apart with the ring of the axe. The split pieces were tossed aside, and Dawn and I would stack them up to season. The dry spruce kindling was piled under cover; it was precious.

The wood rack in the house was loaded with firewood that had been cut a month or so before. But several green chunks were always brought in for the night fire. They would burn low and slowly, and there'd still be coals left the next morning. Then I'd get up and put a couple of big handsful of dry kindling on the coals. On top of that, I'd crisscross split pieces of spruce and birch. In a few minutes the fire would sputter, then roar, as it touched off the bark on the birch wood. It wasn't long before we were sitting with our feet up on the hearth, sipping our breakfast coffee.

Dad had an old saying about firewood — "It warms you twice, once while cutting it, and once while burning it!"

Billy
& Bree

▼▼▼

When our Dawn reached the age of 12, her greatest wish in this whole wide world was to have a beautiful, shiny, fleet-footed horse — preferably a chestnut-colored thoroughbred.

She had more influence than most girls her age; we kept farm animals and had plenty of room. And anyway, a horse would be useful on the homestead.

Dad scouted around and came up with the nearest thing he could find at an affordable price — a cute and fuzzy, sassy little brown and white pony named Billy, free for the keeping.

Billy was an immediate success. His bare back was easy to climb onto, and he was always ready to go. Dawn and Lanny rode him every minute of their spare time. Billy was a friendly fellow who won over the whole family — even me who had always been timid around horses of any color. We let him have the run of the yard with the rest of our livestock.

But Billy had been around.

He learned quickly how to open the latch on the feed house door. And the barn, where we locked up all the animals every evening, was no barrier to him either. We'd wake in the middle of the night to the sound of hoofbeats, and there would be Billy out in the yard, kicking up his heels in the moonlight.

He liked to play hard to catch, too, and required cajoling and pleading to come when he didn't want to.

But Billy was a good help around the homestead. Dad made a harness for him so he could pull toboggan loads of wood. He'd work his heart out for a few cubes of sugar.

The biggest feat Billy performed was the day we brought home a new gas refrigerator. It was March, and the slope from the driveway to the house was covered with slick ice. Harnessed and hitched to a makeshift skid, old Billy dug in his hooves and tugged that 300-pound crate up to the door, huffing and puffing all the way.

He earned a bunch of sugar cubes for that job.

Dawn, meanwhile, had shown that she could love, cherish, and care for a horse. So the next summer, we bought her a beautiful one-year old Welsh buckskin named Bree.

For a year, Dawn trained the horse daily, using methods she found in library books. She taught him commands, trotted him around in a circle holding a long-line rope, and got him used to carrying things on his back — first a feed bag, then a blanket, and finally a saddle.

At last, the day came when Dawn climbed on Bree's back with Dad holding the reins. At first, Bree turned his head around for a moment as if to say "okay." And then off they started, both greenhorns, but willing to practice their new-found skills together.

When Dawn was busy elsewhere, our other horse, Billy, would take the opportunity to teach Bree all his special tricks. Bree learned how to open the feed house door and how to stay just out of reach when someone wanted to put a rope on him.

One day, I drove Lanny over to the clearing to fetch the horses. I watched both horses grazing leisurely, quiet and relaxed, even as Lanny walked toward them. But when they spied the rope in his hand, their ears pricked up and they were on alert. Still, they acted as if they hadn't a care in the world.

When Lanny came within a few feet, the horses moved away a few feet, nonchalantly. Lanny spoke coaxingly and got a little closer. With a shake of his head, Billy trotted off and Bree followed.

Lanny made a rush at them, and off they galloped — but not before Lanny got hold of a few hairs on Billy's mane. That slowed the pony down enough for the boy to jump on his back, Indian-style. As they galloped through the field, Billy following Bree, Lanny leaned sideways, reached out, and grabbed Bree's halter.

The game was over.

The horses allowed themselves to be tied and led home to their barn, acting meek and gentle as they knew they should be, looking so irreproachable it was impossible to scold them.

When our twins outgrew Billy, we gave him to friends with young children. Eventually, he lived with many house-holds, all with plenty of kids. They all loved him — even though I am sure he never got over his mischievous ways.

For the rest of our homestead years, Bree stayed with us. And beyond that, Dawn kept him for many years. He was a good worker, and he did get over much of his naughtiness — when not aided and abetted by Billy.

Homestead Cats

Chena thought he was the only cat in the world. He'd lived on the homestead since he was a kitten, and his memories of his mother and siblings must have been very dim.

He had, for playmates, Bing, Snowball and Harry — three big dogs who were amiable and deferential to him. Outside, Chena was king of the hill. When it was time to come in, he was always first in line by dint of scrambling underneath the dog nearest the door. In the house, he sat closest to the fire or on somebody's lap. He was fed on demand. His existence was one of dignity and comfort, like that of all cats.

But Chena knew there was something missing from his life. On warm spring evenings, he would go wandering down the driveway and into the wilderness, meowing with some unrecognized yearning in his heart. We'd hear him return in the morning, still crying, unfulfilled.

So we got him a kitten — a sleek little black female we called Eartha Kitt.

Chena was awestruck when we opened the shoe box where Eartha was crouched. With squeaky little chirps, he inspected her all over.

Immediately he became her mother.

He washed her thoroughly and then let her "nurse" on his tummy. She slept wound up in his paws. When she awoke, he nudged her to the milk dish and taught her how to lap with her tongue.

As Eartha grew and became more active, the two romped and tumbled together. Chena coached her in the art of fighting, prancing around on his toes with his back and tail up in the air. Outside, they practiced hunting together, lying in wait and pouncing on dead leaves blowing in the breeze.

Sometimes, back by the fire, Eartha wanted to play while Chena wished to nap. To indulge her, he would hang his tail down from the chair and allow her to bat it around. When she jumped up to pester him, he'd hold her down with his paw, and wash her until she relaxed and fell asleep.

He protected her obsessively from the Huskies. One afternoon, as our unsuspecting dog Snowball dreamed by the fire probably chasing rabbits in her sleep, Eartha swiped at the dog's tail. Snowball twitched, turned her head around in surprise, and let out a yip. Chena leapt onto the dog's back, and dug in with all his claws. He rode the terrified animal round and round inside the house until someone opened the door for her to escape.

As time went by, Eartha matured into an elegant cat, and Chena fell in love. He greeted her every time he passed her with a kiss. He backed off from the feeding dish and waited politely when she dined. He watched her with a new kind of adoration in his eyes.

Soon they had a family, and it was Eartha's practice to have Chena baby-sit for a few hours each day. He would lie in the box out in the shed, with kittens crawling all over him, while Eartha hunted.

One day, as Dawn and I sat on the porch, we saw Eartha return from her hunt with a rabbit in her mouth as big as she was. She dragged it up the hill between her legs, stopping every few feet to lay it down and rest. The Huskies, thoroughly cat-trained, sat still as statues by the house and watched, too. When she was out of sight around the corner of the shed, they scrambled down the hill, and sniffed wistfully at the scent of the rabbit in the places where Eartha had set it down.

After a while, Chena and Eartha, their family fed and cared for, came outside to rest. They lay regally in the sunshine looking out over the yard, the hill, and the valley, comfortable in the knowledge that this, along with everyone in it, was their domain.

The Good Earth

▼▲▼▲▼▲▼▲▼▲▼▲▼▲▼▲▼▲▼▲▼▲▼▲▼▲▼▲▼▲▼▲▼▲▼▲

Every homesteader, I believe, has a hidden desire to live off the wild land. In Interior Alaska, that's not practical — especially for people like me who grew up amid canned and frozen foods, and packaged baked goods. And with Dad working in town most days, the bulk of our sustenance had to come from the supermarket.

But as much as we could, we did take advantage of nature's edibles. We consumed moosemeat, of course, whenever we could get it, and caribou, too. One year when a black bear came into the yard looking for farm animals to eat, Dad took it by surprise; we ate the bear instead.

Sometimes, Dad shot rabbits and spruce grouse along the road home from work. In summer's long evening light, they were easy to spot.

Fishing trips to the Copper River supplied us with salmon, and we caught whitefish and grayling in our local streams. What we didn't eat right away was canned or wrapped for the freezer we kept at a friend's house in town. When winter came, we moved it all to nature's big freezer — outside on the front porch.

We tried wild greens we had read about: Lamb's quarters, which grew as weeds in our garden, were delicious when picked early and cooked like spinach. Wild asparagus grew abundantly in the woods, but it was tough and tasted terrible. Young dandelion leaves made a good salad and their roots, boiled up, made a passable coffee.

I'd heard much about Labrador tea plants and picked off their leaves and steeped them, but Dad said, "Phoo! It tastes like swampwater tea!"

And I guess it really did.

In rainy August, wild mushrooms were plentiful; the Orange Bolites were easy to identify. We all enjoyed mushroom soup and stew from recipes I found in an old family cookbook.

We experimented with birch syrup, tapping it from the trees in spring, and boiling it down. In a world catastrophe it would do as a sweetener, we decided, but meanwhile, we'd stick with store-bought sugar and maple syrup.

We tried and tasted, devoured or discarded, all these wild foods.

Mother Nature's great gift to us was berries: raspberries and blueberries, cranberries and rose hips. Our homestead was set in the middle of a bounteous berry land.

Raspberries volunteered themselves all over the berm piles in our 10 acre clearing; there was enough to supply a village. In late July, we started harvesting them, scrambling over the piles, risking our bones as we placed our feet blindly into tangled, rotting limbs and brush.

We scooped the bright red berries into our wire-handled coffee cans.

A few weeks later, the cans were used to pick the blueberry patch just a few miles up the road. The berries there were so abundant that we could sit on the ground and pick half a pail without moving.

Down the road the other way was a thicket of highbush cranberries, just off a path lined with wild rose bushes full of blushing rose hips.

In September, the season's culmination came after the first hard frost, when the lowbush cranberries turned a deep red all over our woods. Clusters of berries snuggled in the green moss around fallen birch logs looked like miniature landscapes for elves or fairies. It was so pleasant to bask there in the autumn sunshine, picking fruit. These were the last days of good weather before blustery winter blew in.

As the days grew shorter, our food cupboards filled. Crocks and Mason™ jars sat alongside containers of commercial foods. Alaska's wilds supplied our table with goodies like moosemeat hamburgers with wild highbush cranberry catsup, and fried spruce grouse served with lowbush cranberry sauce. Blueberry pie, its crust made with lard from the bear, was often served for dessert.

On frosty mornings, we sat down to pancakes covered with pink, fruity rose hip syrup, or toast spread with raspberry jam.

These and other wild things provided a good deal of our diet. Even though we did not live off the land completely, we would not be destitute if suddenly there were no other sources of food.

The earth was the primary source of all that we needed.

ALONG THE ROAD
TO TOWN

The Elliott
Highway

The road that led to our homestead — the Elliott Highway — was pretty, but long. It branched off from the Steese Highway about 10 miles north of Fairbanks in a northwesterly direction.

There were perhaps two dozen cabins, trailers, and Quonset huts along the first 20 miles, but only half of these structures were inhabited. The others were empty and rotting away, some without roofs, their foundations sinking awkwardly into the permafrost below.

Over the next 30 miles, the lonely Elliott climbed over the top of Wickersham Dome — one of the high, rounded hills that cover this region of Interior Alaska — and down through a deep valley, crossing several creeks. It wound around the hills, traversed the river where we got water, and rambled on through birch forests to our hillside.

Past our homestead, the highway continued to Livengood, an abandoned mining town, and finally to Manley Hot Springs, 130 miles from Fairbanks.

The road's surface was gravel, with bumps, humps and hollows that had established themselves over the years. It was quite narrow in some places, especially on steep ascents with sharp outcroppings and sheer drop-offs. There were no guard rails.

In the fall of each year, the highway department erected a sign at 21 Mile. It stated that through the winter, the road would not be maintained beyond that point and that travel would be at one's own risk and peril.

The sign meant what it said; that first winter we had to stay in town.

But when oil was discovered on the North Slope of Alaska, the state built a 300-mile-long ice road from the Elliott to the Slope to haul drilling equipment. For the next few years, part of the road was plowed, but only now and then.

One notable exception was on a stormy day when the plow came all the way to our driveway at 49-1/2 Mile and turned around. The driver said he knew Dad's truck didn't have four-wheel drive and he might have a bad time getting home. In winter, the road would usually have only a double line of wheel tracks on it or, after a fresh snow, would be unmarked, a smooth, white thread trailing through the wilderness.

Worse than the snows that drifted over the highway were the glaciers that formed in the valleys near the creeks. In these places, the road would become covered with slick ice, usually on a slant, which would build up as water seeped over the top and froze. There was an art to driving here — not accelerating nor using the brakes, and holding one's breath, hoping for the best. I would just close my eyes as Dad drove over the glaciers.

Sometimes pioneers can be cowards.

In cold winters, the temperature would fluctuate as we drove over hill and vale, rising in the high terrain and falling as much as 30 degrees down in the lowlands. The truck would actually squeal in misery as the grease and oil in its innards congealed.

We were all glad to get to our home on the hillside.

Most of the year, the quiet highway accommodated state highway workers, a few families who lived out beyond us (who did not commute every day), and weekend adventurers. We always carried emergency gear on the road — blankets and sleeping bags, survival food, matches and a hatchet.

It was not a good road to catch a ride on.

One fellow tried hitchhiking home from town one night. He got a ride as far as 20 Mile, then started walking. At 24 Mile, he got tired, built a campfire in the road, curled up in his bedroll, and went to sleep until someone finally came along and picked him up.

In summertime, we could often tell when someone was coming our way. We would look out across the valley, and see the dust rising from a vehicle many miles away.

In due time, it would pass by us.

As I waited for Dad to come home on late summer nights, I could hear the hum of his engine through the open cabin window as his pickup crossed the rise at 48 Mile. Then, in a few minutes, the sound of the truck door slamming would reverberate up to the house from the driveway below.

I'd know then that Dad was safely home after his one-and-a-half-hour drive over the infamous Elliott Highway.

Shooting on the Road

Usually, there was so little traffic on our road that, if we did hear a vehicle, we strained to see what was coming. But this wasn't true during hunting season.

First came the bird hunters. They drove along the highway looking left and right to see if they could spy fluttering movements in the branches. Whether bird or leaf, whatever it was seemed worth taking a shot at.

There must have been a lot of fluttering between our house and the road because, several times a day, someone would stop to shoot up the hill toward us. Our log cabin was not easy to see from the road, nor were our children who played in the woods. The twins had orders to stand behind trees while I hollered down from the doorway to "please shoot somewhere else."

Most hunters stopped shooting and left, but there were a couple of exceptions.

One evening at dusk, there were a lot of gunshots. Dad was home and shouted down the hill to no avail. Finally, he walked down to the road and found the occupants of three pickups all aiming 22's at a poor little spruce hen who didn't have the sense to fly away.

Fortunately, all the hunters were bad shots. They were bad sports, too, and didn't leave until Dad firmly reminded them about the laws concerning shooting from the roadway onto private property.

On a different occasion, a hunter repeatedly shot toward our hillside. This time, we thought we'd try something different. After one round, I let out a bloodcurdling scream, as if I were mortally wounded. The sounds stopped, a car door slammed, and tires screeched away.

That was the last of that unmindful hunter.

In September, moose season came along and the traffic on the Elliott Highway got heavier. Quite a few hunters chose our gravel pit as the place to sight their rifles. It was a little farther from the house, but Dad usually drove down to let the shooters know that people lived nearby. More times than not, they'd get to visiting, and pretty soon they'd all be up at our house for coffee and to see what a homestead looked like.

We made some friends that way.

By Labor Day weekend, campers, cars and trucks were traveling the road at about three-minute intervals, each one unknowingly just out of sight of the other. Hunters searched diligently for moose as they drove along. (We kept our brown horse securely tied up and out of sight!) The poor moose, if they had wanted to cross the road, would have needed a traffic light.

After moose season closed, the road was ours again. But there were still a few weekend adventurers. One Sunday, our Dawn was on her way home from the clearing with Harry, our Husky dog. A car full of young military men stopped on the roadside, and Dawn secluded herself in the woods. But the soldiers' eyes were on our hapless dog who looked like a wolf silhouetted on an embankment.

"WOLF!" cried one of the boys as rifles were shouldered and aimed.

"HARRY!" shouted Dawn.

"WOOF, WOOF!" barked Harry.

Four surprised young warriors climbed sheepishly back into their car and drove away.

As the days grew shorter, the traffic grew thinner. By the time winter weather set in, we saw fewer tire tracks on the snowy road, and were back to the window to see what was passing by.

Car
Troubles

In Interior Alaska, at 50 or 60 degrees below zero, it takes a lot of preparation to get a vehicle ready for the road.

First, of course, the engine needs warming. In Fairbanks, most cars are equipped with an engine heater; you simply plug the cord into the nearest outlet.

In the bush, it is a different story. One way is to hook a propane bottle to a hose on a weed burner — a long rubber hose with a sort of flame thrower on the end of it. The burner is placed under the vehicle inside a baffle or a piece of old stovepipe, to prevent the flame from coming in direct contact with the engine. Then, the heater is lit and everyone hopes for the best.

Once the engine is started, however, only half the battle is won. Next, the vehicle must be put into motion: the grease around the wheel bearings has probably solidified, and the tires, having taken a set, have flat bottoms. The standard remedy is to shift the vehicle back and forth slowly in the driveway until things loosen up a bit.

One January day Dad was out rocking the pickup back and forth, getting ready to go to work, when suddenly the gear shift stopped working. The truck would not move forward or backward, no matter how he moved the lever.

With no way to get to an automotive shop, there was nothing he could do but remove the steering wheel, pull out the shifting tube, and see what was wrong. Dad did this, brought the whole assembly into the house, and set it on the table. He found the trouble; the stud at the bottom of the shifting tube had sheared off.

What to do? Well, he'd see what he could find.

After rummaging in his tool box, he got an idea and went to find the old nail can. Pulling out two or three nails, he matched one with the broken stub and sawed it to the right length. He popped the nail into place, assembled the tube, put it all back into the truck — and drove off to work.

That wasn't the only time Dad was forced to use makeshift measures.

While driving along the road one day, the engine heated up alarmingly. He stopped the truck, got out, and looked under the hood. He found radiator fluid leaking from the housing of the water pump. Using his jackknife and a piece of green spruce, he made a neat plug for the hole.

Both makeshift repairs remained in place for as long as we had the truck. But sometimes stopgap actions didn't work. Like the time the engine blew up. This happened to our poor old pickup one winter's night when Dad was coming home from work, just a mile and a half from the homestead. Of course, we were in the midst of another cold spell, but the faithful truck made it to the bottom of the driveway before she died.

Dad walked up the hill, came in, and went to bed.

But there we all were — no transportation, no communication. With so little traffic on the road, we certainly couldn't stand down there and freeze, hoping for a chance car to come along.

In the morning, Dad made a big sign that said:

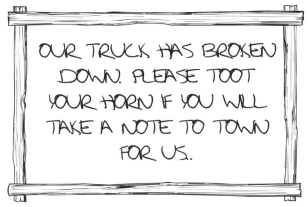

OUR TRUCK HAS BROKEN DOWN. PLEASE TOOT YOUR HORN IF YOU WILL TAKE A NOTE TO TOWN FOR US.

Then he cut a long spruce pole from the woods. He nailed the sign onto it and stuck it in the back of the pickup. The sign reached just out to the road.

In the early afternoon, we heard a "toot-toot" down on the road. I took a note down to some brave adventurers who were out for a drive in that weather and asked them to take it to the preacher at our church.

That night, there was a message for us on the radio that our friend Fred would be out in the morning with a tow bar.

Fred came and hauled Dad and the pickup to town. The preacher and his wife drove out to the homestead with a sack of groceries sent by other friends. Dad was home for the weekend. And, in a few days, the truck was back on the road again with a rebuilt engine.

We knew that Dad would not always be able to fix the truck with things he had on hand. Someday, it would fail us again.

But our good friends, we learned, never would.

Church Around the Wood Stove

After we came to Alaska, we attended a little chapel 10 miles out of Fairbanks. It sat on rocky tailings created years ago by gold dredges working along Goldstream Creek.

Inside, the congregation sat on metal folding chairs on a bare wood floor. The plasterboard walls were painted army-ordinance, pea-soup green. In the rear of the room, a black pot-bellied stove did its best to keep the building warm. Double-thick windows looked over a patch of scrub alder bushes that had managed to take root from the few grains of soil among the rocks.

What a contrast this was to my church back in New York, with its velvet cushioned pews and stained-glass windows. The minister there dressed in a satin-trimmed black robe and preached through a microphone from a large, elaborate chancel.

At our chapel in Alaska, Brother Crook — the only man wearing a necktie — stood behind a rickety table to speak.

In my old church, I had felt important attending committee meetings with prominent people in our city. We had membership drives, pledge seasons, and well-organized programs for youth and adults.

At the chapel, everyone was important. And when someone needed help, money and support always came through.

Brother Crook liked to visit the homestead with his wife. Fifty years before in his childhood in Wisconsin, he had lived a life similar to our own. Wood fires and water buckets were familiar to him. He liked being around the farm and once, when Dad was away, helped deliver three baby goats, one of them breech. He liked to talk about old times but on every visit, at one point, he would take out his worn black Bible and deliver a little lesson. The gospel was never forgotten.

Sometimes the whole assembly would come out to the homestead for a potluck. We'd all eat from paper plates on our laps; the cabin would be overflowing. People sat on stools and benches, rungs of the ladder leading upstairs, and on the kitchen sink. Afterwards, our gospel songs would resound through the log walls and into the woods beyond.

We didn't go to church regularly. It was 100 miles round trip. But on Friday nights, we often stopped by the Bible study on our way home from shopping in town. My favorite meetings were those on cold winter nights when we'd all sit in a circle around the potbellied stove to keep warm. There, in a quiet voice, Brother Crook would talk about what the Bible said, referring to verses he knew by heart, while we followed along in our own books. He turned the Scriptures into personal messages.

In that little chapel, I learned that churches are not made from stained-glass, steeples, and successful fundraisers — but from the love, faith and commitment in our hearts.

The Day
of the Moose

▼▼▼▼▼▼▼▼▼▼▼▼▼▼▼▼▼▼▼▼▼▼▼▼▼▼▼▼▼▼▼▼▼▼▼▼▼

Winter had been severe. We had four feet of snow on the ground, and for over a month, the temperature had been 40 to 50 degrees below zero.

Finally on a bright morning when there was a break in the weather, we drove over to the Steese Highway to visit our friends Fred and Jo. Every few miles along the way, we saw a moose or two browsing, floundering belly-deep in snow, their backs white with frost. They seemed nearly helpless as they struggled to get food; we felt sorry for the poor things.

When we got to Fred's driveway, Dad gunned the engine of the old Ford to make a rush up the slippery, steep hill. Fred had packed down a track in the snow with his 4-by-4, but our two-wheel-drive pickup barely made it up the first curve.

As we rounded the bend, in front of us stood a young bull moose, as surprised to see us as we were to see him. Dad tapped the horn, and the moose trotted up the drive a little way and around the next bend.

But we'd lost our traction and had to back down the drive to get another start.

We drove up again, wheels spinning, and made it a little farther. But there, just around the next bend, was the moose, congratulating us for making it that far.

▶ 125

There in front of us stood a young bull.

Another toot prodded him on, as we backed down a second time and tried once more. You guessed it; waiting around the last curve was the young moose.

Finally, we all made it up to the house — us tooting and the moose trotting. Fred and Jo, watching the action from their porch, held their sides with laughter and shot pictures of us and our adversary.

This was too much for the little bull. He turned on us and stood up on his back legs with obvious intentions of slamming his front hooves down on our hood.

Dad geared into reverse and backed up.

Then the moose, tired of it all, turned his hind end to us and wallowed off into the woods.

We spent our day making sausage from a leg of a moose that Fred had shot in the fall. The men hacked the meat off the bone and cut it into cubes, and Jo and I cranked it through the grinder three times — two parts moose meat, one part suet. We mixed up a bowl of it with some spices for a test batch, and fried little patties to pass around.

"Too mild; try again."

We added some sage and cooked up more patties.

"Very good. But let's taste more to make sure!"

Our product was flawless.

We calculated pounds of meat by the fistful and pinches of spices by the spoonfuls and ended up with four dishpans of savory sausage. We wrapped packages in waxed paper, newspaper, and sealed them with tape. A box full went into the truck for us.

Starting down the driveway that evening, we were gratified that no moose was waiting for us. But when we turned out onto the road, we found a full-sized cow moose with her yearling calf taking up the middle of the highway. Close up she was enormous; she didn't look helpless at all.

Dad eased the truck behind her and tried to pass; she turned herself broadside and blocked us.

"Okay, Lady, it's your road," said Dad, following a safe distance behind.

Soon they'll turn off, we thought. But Mama Moose thought differently. She wasn't going to wade through those high snow berms with her baby!

After a mile or so, Dad stopped the truck and turned off the headlights. Maybe they would be less nervous and go on their way. A few minutes later, he turned the lights on again.

They were in front of us, resting.

Dad tooted to no avail. Then he thought he had the answer — his 357 magnum Smith and Wesson. He leaned out the window and fired high into the air.

The cow about-faced and marched our way. Advancing to the truck, she glared down at us through the windshield, her wild eyeballs glittering. We looked up at her and got the message. She was fully in charge. Dad valiantly retreated.

For five miles, at a respectable distance and in second gear, we followed the pair down the road. Finally, at the end of a bridge railing, they found a break in the snow berm and turned off the road.

Once again masters of our fate, we drove the rest of the way home, looking forward to cooking up the box of moose sausage tucked in the back of the truck.

Dogs &
Wolf Snares

snowball wouldn't stop barking.

We covered our heads with our blankets and tried to sleep. But all night long, she'd been woofing off and on. Dad had been to the door three times to peer out at the woods surrounding our cabin; he'd seen nothing amiss.

Dogs. Bah!

Yesterday, Bing had run off somewhere and wasn't back by bedtime; we were getting uneasy about him. And now Snowball simply wouldn't shut up.

Dad went to the door once more. "Be quiet, Snowball!" he hollered.

The white Husky, instead of dutifully hushing, climbed the porch steps and barked in Dad's face. Yapping excitedly, she ran down the steps, down the hill a little way, turned back, and barked some more.

"I believe she wants me to follow her!" said Dad.

He dressed quickly, putting on his boots and parka. He walked down the hill in the early morning twilight.

Snowball ran ahead, then came back to make sure Dad was coming along. She led him along the path, across the road, and down about a quarter of a mile through the snow to the lower part of the 160-acres.

There, in a grove of alders, was Bing — his neck held tightly in the noose of a wolf snare. A piece of moosemeat bait lay nearby. Dad, who always had a pocket full of tools, snapped the wire with his cutting pliers and freed the dog. Bing showed his gratefulness with jumps and kisses. The two dogs and Dad returned to the cabin in triumph; I got up and put the coffee on.

After breakfast, Dad wrote a note to the trapper which said:

YOU ARE TRAPPING ON PRIVATE PROPERTY, AND YOU HAVE CAUGHT MY DOG. PLEASE REMOVE ALL YOUR TRAPS IN THIS AREA.

It wasn't surprising that someone had made this mistake. Our homestead was far from any other habitation, and our house could not be seen easily from the road. The dogs' large footprints in the snow could look like they belonged to wolves.

Dad, with Snowball and Bing following, retraced his steps through the woods and nailed the note to the tree the snare was tied to. Then he climbed the hill to the house again. In a few minutes, Snowball trotted up behind him — but Bing didn't.

Down the hill tramped Dad again, following the now well-packed trail through the snow to the alder grove.

Bing was caught in another wolf snare.

A second time, Dad released him and, after a careful search, found a dozen more snares and pieces of moose bait under the snow. Dad closed the loop on each trap, and one last time, they returned home, safe and sound and well-exercised.

The trapper must never have come back. The next autumn, the note still hung on the tree, and the deadly wires — fortunately harmless by then — lay among the drying leaves on the ground.

When It's
Springtime in Alaska

▼▼▼▼▼▼▼▼▼▼▼▼▼▼▼▼▼▼▼▼▼▼▼▼▼▼▼▼▼▼▼▼▼▼▼▼▼▼▼

In late April, as the snow on our hillside started to melt, water trickled down our paths and driveway in little rivulets, running its course over the route of least resistance.

Dad, the kids and I, using any excuse to be out in the spring sunshine, would dabble and dig with sticks and shovels, building little dams to divert the flow away from the driveway and walks. But after a while, the dams gave way, and the water found its own channel. Bubbling merrily along again, it flowed down the drive to the foot of the hill.

As time went on, the water sank deeper into the ground, the driveway softened, and it became impossible to bring our truck up to the house. The walkways were two inches deep in mud, and we had to wear our "break-up" boots to do our chores.

When we came inside, we left the grimy boots by the door, even just to drop a single load of firewood. But everything in the house got muddy anyway. Our clothes were always dirty, so we dressed in our rattiest jeans and sweatshirts.

We looked like muck farmers, which I guess, we were.

But after a couple of weeks, the juicy mud dried to a fragile firmness, and we were able to step outside without changing our footwear. The wild crocuses came into bloom, and the trees started leafing out.

It was time to think spring.

So, on our next trip to Fairbanks for supplies, we dressed to the nines. I still remember the beige sandals I wore with my flower-print dress.

In town, the morning was sunny and warm. But at noon the sky clouded over, and by mid-afternoon it was raining. We ducked into stores to shop as Dad loaded up the back of the truck. On top of the pile went a brand-new wheelbarrow.

In the evening, we went to Bible study at church. The other members of the congregation, who had not dressed for the occasion in the sunny dawn, wore sensible sweaters and rain boots. I felt like a tulip among them and would have given anything for the warmth of one of my old sweatshirts at home. I'd been rushing the season, I realized.

Late that evening, as we drove the 50 miles to our homestead, we saw that the rain had turned to snow at the higher elevations. By the time we reached home, there were four inches on the ground. We turned into the entrance of our homestead and found that the bottom had gone out of the driveway again. This meant we'd have to carry our groceries and supplies up the hill.

Grudgingly, we got out and went to the back of the truck to pick up bags of groceries.

But wait! There was that new wheelbarrow!

Dad loaded it with bags and started pushing it up the long hill. I scurried on ahead, trying to step lightly through the snow in my sandals. I was on my way to light the lamps, start a fire, and hold the door open for the others.

But the wheelbarrow was too heavy to push up the hill; it bogged down in the snow. Dad called me back. He tied three lengths of rope to the frame and gave the ends to me and the kids. We pulled and he pushed, and the wheelbarrow made its way slowly up the path.

My sandals squished through the snow into the mud below. But what matter, I thought; it was late, we were tired, and we always pulled together on the homestead.

Then from the rear came, *On You Huskies, Mush!* along with a wicked laugh.

That was the end of family harmony for the day.

It didn't return until the next afternoon, after the snow had melted away, when we sat on the porch steps in the sunshine, and watched springtime burst forth in the woods again.

Rabbits

vvvvvvvvvvvvvvvvvvvvvvvvvvvvvvvvvvvvvvvvvv

Back in the early '70s, our area was overrun with snow-shoe hares.

We'd see them as we drove between our homestead and town — little groups playing on the road — sometimes three or four, sometimes a dozen or more. It got to be a game to count them, and we'd often observe three or four hundred on the journey.

Rabbits were good to eat.

Many a time Dad brought home a pair he'd shot on the way from work. Overnight, he'd put them to soak in saltwater. The next day, I'd make stew. Simmered on the back of the stove for three or four hours, and served with dumplings and gravy, snowshoe hare was one of our favorite homestead meals.

Our dogs liked to supplement their diets with rabbit-on-the-run. They'd sit on their haunches in the yard, alert, their eyes roving the woods. When one spied a movement in the brush, the race was on — with much woofing and scrambling. Usually the rabbit escaped, but now and then a dog came home with a furry carcass which he devoured greedily in front of the envious others.

Rabbits

The rabbits kept multiplying. White in winter, brown in the summer, they overpopulated the countryside and moved into people's back yards. Gardeners hated them. Plants started in the spring and tended lovingly for months in the house, fell victim to bunny teeth when they were set out in June.

No fencing seemed effective. We all fretted over our vegetables and speculated on new schemes to keep Brer Rabbit away — to little avail.

And still, they frolicked on the roadway.

It was hard to keep from hitting them. A driver had to bear in mind that it was not worth going over a cliff to avoid a rabbit; they darted around so fast that they were impossible to avoid anyway.

One winter's night, Dad came upon an interesting sight. There on the road before him was a dead rabbit, ears flattened down, feet out straight.

Suddenly, the rabbit jumped.

Dad slowed down. The rabbit jumped again — about a foot across the road. Dad stopped and got out. Across another foot of road went the rabbit. Dad looked closely and, underneath it, saw a little weasel catching its breath, resting up for another jump.

There are strange things to be seen in Alaska!

But Nature has a way of keeping her world in balance. The hare's predator, the lynx, moved into the area. We'd often see one along the road, frozen momentarily in the glare of our headlights. Staring back at us, it would slink with supple grace into the darkness on its long spindly legs.

One morning, we had a lynx in our yard, and Harry Dog had it treed high in a birch. This lynx was not welcome; we had too many chickens and goats running around loose. Dad shot it and made me a beautiful hat from its fur.

On winter weekends, lynx trappers in pickup trucks loaded with snowmobiles drove out the highway from town. They parked in every available pullout and made snow trails over hill and valley, setting and checking traps. It was a profitable business; raw lynx hides brought over 100 dollars. Some people made good livings on the trapline.

But after a couple of years, when the rabbits diminished, the lynx moved to more abundant hunting grounds and so did the trappers.

The rabbits had reached the low point in their cycle; over the next six or seven years, we rarely saw one.

Fishing
at Chitina

I n late June, when the kings and red salmon ran up the Copper River by Chitina, we packed up the family truck for the nine-hour trip to go dipnetting.

At the homestead, it was usually very hot that time of year. It was hard to remember to pack wool shirts and heavy sweaters. But we had learned, by painful experience in the cold, wet and windy Copper River Valley, how necessary these things would be. We also threw in warm hats,  socks, gloves and raincoats. (One time I forgot the raincoats — we all walked around wearing green garbage bags with slits for neck and armholes!)

One year, we loaded the camper shell on the pickup with food, clothing, and a 16-quart canner. On top, we tied a huge dipnet made from a spruce pole and chicken wire. Four across the front seat of the cab, we traveled the 350 miles to the little town with the big reputation for salmon.

When we arrived, we parked among the other trucks and campers as close as we could to the riverbank. Dad wasted no time. He got out of the truck, put on his hip boots, grabbed his net, and stepped out into the water to start dipping.

It seemed impossible that any living thing could survive in that silty, swift-moving river. After the first half hour of sweeping his net, Dad was ready to give up for a while. But he felt a bump on the net and pulled in a fine 10-pound red. A few minutes later, a 50-pound king hit his net. Dad scooped it up, while we helped with the net handle. As soon as the big fish hit the beach, it headed back for the water, biting through the chicken wire, and humping along the gravel. But Dad laid down on top of it, while I fetched the hunting knife.

Soon, the king was conquered.

Other fishermen emerged from their campers and tents and lined the river, also sweeping their dipnets for salmon. That run lasted a couple of hours, and then stopped. One or two tenacious hopefuls continued to fish staunchly out in the cold, while the rest of the netters stayed inside their warm shelters. From time to time, they would peek out to see when the next run started, and then they'd all line up again to catch another few.

This cycle continued all day and through the ever-light nighttime. During the lapses, Dad and Lanny cut up our fish and Dawn and I filled sterile jars for the canner. Then my job was to watch the pressure as the canner steamed away on a gas hot plate inside our camper shell.

We packed a few of the fish in a brown sugar and salt marinade for smoking after we got home. The last batch of fish was earmarked for freezing; we packed them in a 30-gallon plastic garbage can.

When we'd fished our limit, we took off for Fairbanks again, stopping only at a mountainside glacier to collect ice for the garbage can. Driving along tired and dirty, we stripped away layers of clothing as we drew closer and closer to our homestead. I dozed, dreaming of slabs of iridescent red meat and bountiful rushing waters.

It was always good to arrive home with our winter's supply of fish.

Forest Fires

I used to love the long hot days in June and July. Clear blue skies could dominate the weather pattern for weeks, interrupted only by scattered thunderstorms.

It was a northern paradise.

Besides producing lovely summer days, this weather was perfect for forest fires. The burning sun made the ground cover warm to the touch and dry as tinder in the woods. Any electrical storm could touch off a tree and create a devastating inferno.

We were exceedingly careful on the homestead, not allowing even a spark that might ignite our surroundings in an instant. However, thousands of square miles around us were as dry as we were, and sooner or later, the day would come when we'd get a whiff of smoke in the air. The fire that produced it might be 60 or 80 miles away, but still the acrid smell was nerve-wracking.

The forest fire season was upon us.

If the dry weather kept up, more fires would start, and the air around us would turn a hazy blue-gray color. Eventually, the stench would come through the windows, permeating everything in the house. Even the clothes in the closet smelled like smoke, and we had a constant smoky taste in our mouths.

One summer was particularly bad. The smoke from several large fires filled the air and settled in all the lowlands. We went shopping in Fairbanks, and as we drove home over Wickersham Dome, we could not see any of the terrain in the approaching valleys. We had no idea if the smoke ahead was from a new local fire, or if it came from far away. There was nothing to do but continue on, hoping for the best. When we reached home, we were thankful to see our house still safe and standing.

We were on our own out there; we had no neighbors or means of communication. Dad bought us an old reliable car we could escape with if a fire started nearby while he was at work. We prayed that the worst would not happen, but it was unnerving to wonder if a careless smoker might toss a butt out of a car window and start a blaze.

For days on end, the weather pattern stayed the same, but it was no longer hot; the smoke from those blistering fires blocked out the sun and brought an unseasonable chill to the air. We started wearing sweaters around the house.

Finally, one morning, we woke to a steady rain on the roof. Before the day was over it was coming down in torrents, and by evening, the air outside smelled fresh and clean. The radio weatherman predicted that the wet cold front could stay around a while.

Now we could enjoy a cozy fire in our Franklin stove. It was perfectly safe — even a burning ember thrown out on the saturated ground cover would have quickly fizzled in the sogginess.

We no longer thought about forest fires and soon, during that rainy spell, we longed for those hot, dry, wonderful sunny days to return once again.

Tale of
an Adventurer

▼▼

A bout five or six miles down the road, a long-abandoned log cabin was set back in the woods. Inside, it had a table and chair, a wooden bunk, and a few odds and ends. The door worked, but the windows were open to the air outside.

Every couple of years, someone would "squat" there for a month or two, trying out the fantasy of living off the Alaska wilderness.

One summer day, an ex-Marine from Kansas brought his duffel out the highway and dropped in at our house. He'd just arrived in Alaska the week before, but he wanted to start right away to become an Alaska Sourdough. He was looking for a place to live; we told him about the cabin and he settled in.

After a few days of experiencing cabin life, he wanted to explore his surroundings. One of the odds and ends in his cabin was an old baseball bat. Someone had told him that spruce grouse — a kind of slow-witted game bird that populated the area — were good to eat and easy to catch. They even stood still when approached by hunters. Why, he was told, a person could kill them with a shovel — or a baseball bat. So that, our friend determined, was why there was a baseball bat in the cabin.

Early in the afternoon, dressed in a light jacket and a baseball cap, bat in hand, he trekked through the woods behind his house. After a couple of hours of hiking, he turned back toward home. The sky was clouding up and it looked like rain.

But soon, he realized, he wasn't going the right way. Nothing in the woods looked familiar.

He was lost.

Not wanting to panic, he set out in what he thought was the right general direction. After a while, he came to a little stream and walked along it, knowing enough to follow its course.

Then, it started to rain.

Our adventurer wasn't dressed for this and he quickly got cold. Fear set in. Suddenly, there was a loud crashing sound in the brush nearby. It must be a moose, he thought, or even a bear!

Thoroughly frightened, he stepped into the little creek and splashed along noisily, beating the brush alongside with his bat and hollering loudly, trying to scare the beasts away.

The stream led to a small river, which the wanderer correctly guessed to be one he'd seen from the road — the one that we told him he could get water from. It would cross under the highway, but which direction would that be?

Unluckily, the poor man chose upstream. After an hour, he realized he was wrong and turned back. The trip was tortuous in the rain and it was dark when he finally came to the bridge.

By this time, he was so demoralized, he headed in the wrong direction on the road; he didn't realize this until he came to a milepost sign; he turned around.

Late that night, as we were coming home from town, we saw a strange-looking fellow with his cap bill pulled down over his face. He was carrying a baseball bat as he walked along the road in the rain. He seemed to be heading for a party of campers parked in the gravel parking lot by the river. Judging from the sight of him, it must have been some party!

The next day, Dad dropped in to see our new neighbor on his way to work. The poor fellow related his story from his bed, where he was nursing his aching body from his misadventures. He said he never did find a grouse.

A few nights later, a black bear came wandering through our neighbor's yard. Curious, it stuck its head through the open window, waking the man up.

The next morning, our neighbor moved out.

Waking him up!

HOME SWEET HOMESTEAD

Scared!

At first, when we moved to our homestead and lived in tents, I was scared. Scared of everything.

I was scared of bears. There must be some roaming around nearby, I thought. Surely one would come to our camp some night, sniffing around, looking for the food I'd stashed away in a metal drum. He'd claw at the drum until he got to the food; then he'd claw at the tent till he got to me. Each night I'd lie in my sleeping bag waiting for Dad to come home from work, and I'd listen for bears.

Well, as always, Dad came home from work at midnight, and a bear never did come. We moved into our sturdy log cabin, and I stopped being afraid of bears.

Then I was scared of fire. We had a cantankerous wood stove I knew nothing about. With winter coming on, what would my little children and I do if the cabin burned down? There was no other shelter — except the outhouse down the path. Lying in bed, I envisioned the three of us sitting on the two-holer, shivering and terrified, waiting for Dad to come home at midnight.

Well, through the winter, I learned to tend our wood stove. Dad always came home, and I stopped being afraid of fire.

Scared!

Then I was scared of what might happen to Dad on the way home from work. He had many lonely miles to travel and, if he was 10 minutes late, I panicked with visions of horrors on the road.

But soon, I'd hear the truck door slam and hear his footsteps on the path. The cabin door would open, and I felt like there was nothing to be afraid of in the whole world.

But one spring night, Dad didn't come home.

Midnight passed, then one o'clock. I lay on the bed, the clock by my side, listening for the truck door to slam. But the only sound was the ticking of the clock.

Two o'clock passed. I tried to think of logical reasons why he hadn't come home, or why he hadn't sent word on the radio: The truck wouldn't start, he had to work an extra shift, somebody else had an emergency and he had to help out.

At three o'clock, I gave in to terror. The worst had happened, I was sure of it.

By four a.m., my senses dulled by tiredness, pushed my body into an uneasy sleep. But at 5:30 I was up, stoking the fire, making coffee, and looking out the window toward the road at the foot of the hill.

I listened to the seven o'clock news. No accidents reported. I got the children up, and we had breakfast. We did our chores and started work on correspondence lessons.

At noon, I listened again to the news.

Certainly if he'd been in an accident, someone would have found him by now. But, no — just reports of war and gore, murder and mayhem, far away from our world.

I decided to take a nap. Surely there was a simple reason why Dad had stayed in town; I was foolish to be worried.

Drifting off, I felt Dawn shake my shoulder. "Mommy,

there's a state trooper car stopped down by the road."

My stomach bounced up against my heart, which was pounding at my throat. We had never seen a state trooper on our road before!

My muscles turned to jelly; it was with the utmost effort I sat myself up and got out of bed.

I seemed to float down the path, feeling like a fluttering moth headed toward a flame. The white state patrol car shot its red lights at my glazed eyes. The blue-dressed trooper, looming up in front of the lights, was tall and frightening. On his face was an expression of...of what?

His face was pleasant, his words unconcerned.

"Hullo there. I'm the new trooper assigned to this road. I'm going to be patrolling out here once a week or so, and I thought it would be a good idea to meet you folks. Now, if there's anything I can do for you...?"

That trooper never knew why I was so giddy when I asked him up to the cabin for a cup of coffee. I didn't tell him about my fears. No news was good news and Dad was okay, I knew it.

During the afternoon, I put my thoughts in order. Our life at the homestead was too precious to be ruled by fear. From then on, I would face each day as I came to it, and stop being afraid of what might happen.

That evening, almost relaxed, I counted the minutes till midnight. Right on time the truck door slammed, footsteps came up the path, and the door to the cabin opened. Dad walked in, weary from working three shifts, tired from trying to catnap on the seat of the truck between shifts.

He was as glad to be home as I was to have him there.

Now there was nothing to be afraid of in the world.

A Tall,
Cool Drink

vvvvvvvvvvvvvvvvvvvvvvvvvvvvvvvvvvvvvvvvvvvv

O n summer days, when the temperature climbed toward 90 degrees, we liked to stretch out in our lawn chairs under the trees in the yard.

The breeze, though it came in half-hearted little puffs, made a pleasant, cool sound in the birch leaves. The dim, shady woods beyond the yard gave an illusion of coolness, too. And the fact that before long, this very spot would be deep and frozen, had its own chilling effect.

But in our unrefrigerated world, the tall, tepid drinks in our hands never helped us conjure refreshing visions. If it was 86 degrees outside, so were our drinks.

Our drinking water, which came from the spring, was carried in jugs for two hours in the back of the pickup, arriving home warm and tasteless.

So, we devised ways to doctor it up. A package of drink mix helped — that was never improved by chilling anyway. But its sickly sweet taste was not very thirst-quenching.

Dad remembered a concoction called "Schwitzel" that the farm ladies in New York brought out in big pitchers to the hayfield workers. It was flavored with vinegar, water, ginger and sugar.

He mixed some up for us. It sure had a lot of zap! But it didn't fool me; I still longed for a tall, cool drink.

As time went by, things improved on the homestead. We put a small addition on the cabin and installed a 55-gallon drum in the ground beneath a trapdoor in the floor. Things to be cooled went into a basket which was lowered to the bottom of the drum, and a super-sized plastic bag of insulating green moss was stuffed down over it. One had to lie on the floor to reach in for the basket, but it was worthwhile to get something cool to sip on.

By this time, we had learned how to make root beer. We'd bought a bottle capper and a box of caps at the hardware store, and begged and scrounged old beer bottles (the only kind that would accept the snap-on caps) from our friends.

In a large wash pan, I would make a big batch by mixing a 29-cent bottle of root beer concentrate, a couple of pounds of sugar, and a spoonful of yeast with water. The kids took turns funneling it into the bottles and snapping the tops down with the capper (by far their favorite job). We'd store the bottles in a warm place for a few days to let the beer work, and then put them down in our oil-drum cooler.

On hot summer days, we'd dig down for the bottles, and take them out to our lawn chairs in the yard — delectable, cool and satisfying!

But the oil drum was not quite cold enough to keep the root beer from brewing a little more; it could become quite effervescent. So, when we wanted root beer, we'd take a large bowl out with us to the yard. As we opened each bottle, we stood back and a fountain of bubbles would froth up from the neck like Old Faithful. Nothing was wasted, however. We drank half the beer from the bottle and the other half from the bowl.

Some years later, we bought a propane refrigerator. It kept things consistently cold and even had a little place to freeze ice cubes. That allowed for iced tea and lemonade, and somehow, we got out of the habit of making root beer.

It was a shame, because nothing ever tasted so good as those first cool drinks we drank in our lawn chairs out in the yard.

Long-Distance School

Every September, at the same time big yellow school buses would swallow up the city children, several big brown boxes arrived at the homestead from the Alaska State Correspondence School in Juneau.

Unpacking them was as much fun as opening gifts on Christmas. Brand-new pads and pencils, fresh crayons, and intriguing paraphernalia for scientific experiments dazzled the kids and filled them with inspiration for the coming year. Textbooks were perused for a short while, then arranged tidily on the bookshelf under the globe of the world to await the first day of lessons.

Meanwhile, I'd scan the *Home Teacher's Manual* with some diffidence, trying to dig back deep into my memory. What was a predicate nominative? How did one pronounce "Copernicus" or "Ptolemy?" How did protons and electrons work? I wished I had paid more attention during my own school days years ago.

Nevertheless, we started the school year eagerly. We allotted five or six hours a day to studies, scheduling a long midday break so that homestead chores could be done during the short hours of winter daylight.

Much of the instruction took place in front of the Franklin stove, with the three of us trying to fathom the intricacies of mathematics or discovering together the wonders of the earth and the universe. That's also where we shared assigned books of classic literature, breathlessly awaiting Darnay's fate in *A Tale of Two Cities*, or rooting for Rachel in *Ivanhoe*, or appreciating the beauty of *Birches* (which could have been the ones in our own yard) with Robert Frost.

Lessons were done on the dining table under the Aladdin™ lamp. There, I could mix home teaching with homemaking and often dictated a spelling test from the kitchen stove. But sometimes lunch had to wait for the answer to "how many tons of ensilage a farmer could store in a silo."

Teaching often continued through mealtime. Unlike me, Dad seemed to remember everything he had learned in school and could expound at length on early astronomers and how electricity works. He made education an everyday topic of conversation, which helped foster Lanny's and Dawn's yearning to learn.

Every four weeks there were unit tests. Though daily lessons were often read over and corrected by the twins from answer books, unit tests were kept in a manila envelope not to be looked at until testing day arrived. Then it was the time for truth; either the test was passed or the unit was repeated.

The completed tests were sent to Juneau to an advisory teacher, who checked them and wrote long letters of comment.

She added personal notes and really seemed interested in her charges out in the bush. She was our authority — teacher, principal, and advisor, all in one, and our only link to formal schooling. Her classroom extended from Petersburg to the Colville River delta.

Every spring, the Correspondence School sent copies of a yearbook called *Scattered Chatter*, which was full of pictures and stories from students all over Alaska. We read avidly about other families who schooled at home like we did. Many were fishermen from the Southeast; others were trappers, park rangers, bush-business people, or homesteaders like us.

In the '70s much of the correspondence education was transferred from the state to the regional school districts. Each month, correspondence supervisors traveled to oversee their students' work.

That was a real improvement.

No one goes to school in our little log cabin anymore. But I'll bet the spirits of Dickens and Copernicus still echo through the confines of those old log walls.

Golden Days
of Autumn

F all comes to our state earlier than most places in the world. As summer draws to a close, many Alaskans are still in the middle of building projects, camping trips, or watching their gardens grow.

Then one sunny afternoon, a chilly breeze creeps down the back of your neck and you feel the need for a sweater. If you've lived through other Alaska summers, you also feel a strong urgency about that unfinished project, or the small pile of wood by the campfire, or those vegetables still flourishing in the garden rows.

Sure enough, by evening, the temperature has gone down to the 30s, and by morning, there is a frost.

Suddenly, the summer is gone.

Down in the valleys, scrub bushes have turned a deep red overnight, and on the hillsides the birch leaves, not to be left behind, have changed posthaste to gold. Soon the leaves start falling, filling the air with color, making a carpet of yellow on the ground, and giving credence to the Interior's nickname "The Golden Heart of Alaska."

In September, the Elliott Highway was always beautiful. Bright yellow birches and deep green spruces made a kaleidoscope of colors along the way. Photographers, pickers and hunters prowled the road looking to harvest the season's last bounty. Out beyond our homestead, miners cleaned their sluice boxes, delving into the riffles for their year's yield of gold.

Much farther to the north by Prudhoe Bay, huge rigs kept drilling for black gold — oil — deep beneath the surface of the earth, boding change for us in the future.

Our homestead life was coming into its own autumn. Dawn and Lanny were growing up. It wouldn't be too many years before they were looking to their own interests and becoming independent.

Dawn had, by this time, taken an interest in cooking. She loved to experiment with new recipes, especially when one of her girlfriends came to visit. All afternoon they would giggle together in the kitchen — and then come up with a gourmet meal for us.

But Dawn was also becoming a very attractive young lady. On weekends, young fellows came from town to "help out" on the homestead. They chopped firewood, pretentiously if not efficiently, and stepped into the house with mighty armloads to dump into the wood rack near where Dawn was cooking. At mealtime, they would sit by her, some vaunting their virtues, others gazing silently, cow-eyed at her, all trying to make a good impression.

While Dawn didn't have the same opportunities as city schoolgirls, she did have plenty of fellows to look over and discard.

Lanny had taken a great interest in electricity (maybe because he saw so little of it over the years!) In time, we purchased a small, portable generator, and he and Dad strung the first electrical wire to the house. After that, Lanny made plans for, and eventually installed, a whole network of lines, complete with plugs and outlets.

Lanny's friends came to visit also, but theirs was a boys' world. They'd get the daily chores done in jig time, and then go to renovate, in their own way, the old trapper's cabin by the clearing.

By the time Lanny was a young teenager, he used the traps we had found in a nearby tree to set up his own trapline. The hides of the thick-furred marten he caught brought him a very good price, and taught him a lot about being self-sufficient in the wilderness.

In those days, as we watched our children grow and flourish, Dad and I found it hard to think about the time when they would be going off on their own.

Instead, we chose to sit back and enjoy that golden time of autumn when all is so fragile and dear.

The First Snow

▼▼▼▼▼▼▼▼▼▼▼▼▼▼▼▼▼▼▼▼▼▼▼▼▼▼▼▼▼▼▼▼▼▼▼▼

The first snow at the homestead usually fell sometime in October, silently in the night.

Even before our eyes were fully open in the morning, we could tell it had come. The ceiling in the bedroom was lighter than the morning before; there was no sound outside, no sigh of wind. The world seemed to be saying "Hush."

Outside the door, white snow covered everything — the ground, the barn roof, the fence rails, the tree limbs, and the seat on the swing. The two cats, waiting to go out for their morning ritual, stopped affronted at the door sill; they had to be nudged out with a foot. Their own feet were picked up and shaken with disdain at the cold white stuff, and they only scurried off in hauteur when the dogs tore around the corner of the house during their first frolic in the snow.

Out on the road, the gravel surface, so rough and bumpy in the summertime, would turn into a highway as smooth as pavement.

On this day, winter chores started: Sweep the porch, shovel the paths so that gobs of snow would not be brought into the house by our feet, and wipe up around the wood rack by the stove. No matter how well the snow was brushed off the firewood outside, icy little chunks would remain, melt and drip onto the floor. The fires would take more tending; the heavy air outside would try to push the smoke to the ground. Hopefully, everything had been picked up in the yard (an annual September chore) because nothing would be found until spring.

Throughout the day, the lovely, smooth blanket of snow would be desecrated by footprints — trails crisscrossing themselves in the yard. But the snow yard, where I would shovel snow into buckets to melt for wash water, was out of bounds.

When the first snow fell, it was time to burn the brush piles built up from tree cuttings during the past year. Now it was perfectly safe to have a bonfire anywhere in the woods. With matches and an armload of newspaper and kindling, I would set off for the scraggly heaps of old birch limbs and spruce boughs. I always asked for this pleasant job. It took a whole afternoon to do — keeping the flames up, throwing the outer branches into the center of the fire, sitting and cogitating, comfortable and warm out there in the snow.

Snow made wood-hauling easier. In fact, stacks of firewood waited up on the hill to be brought down on the toboggan. Insulating snow would soon pile up against the base of our cabin and keep out winter drafts; and the thick, white coverlet on the roof would help keep heat inside.

In the evening, we would have something cozy like grilled cheese and cocoa for supper. Then we'd get the catalogs out and look for new boots for Lanny and Dawn. Christmas was coming. Maybe Dad would get us a new snowmobile this year!

Finally, at the end of our first day in a new white world, the long winter night found us snugly settled into our beds (with visions of snowmachines dancing in some heads). The two cats stretched out gratefully by the fire, and winter boots sat, unfamiliar, by the door. Outside, the dogs lay curled up with their noses tucked under their tails.

It had started to snow again.

Old-Time Christmas

▼▼▼▼▼▼▼▼▼▼▼▼▼▼▼▼▼▼▼▼▼▼▼▼▼▼▼▼▼▼▼▼▼▼▼▼▼

Christmas on the homestead was like a picture from an old-fashioned storybook. We were sure to have snow, and, miles away from anyplace, our hillside slumbered in silence. The boughs of the spruce trees were dressed in winter finery, and the white-barked birch trees glistened in the moonlight of the long winter nights.

Out back in the barn, fuzzy animals ate from mangers and slept on beds of hay.

All year round, our little cabin looked Christmasy with its green moss chinking peeking out between logs. The sharp crackle of the fire and the soft glow of the kerosene lamps completed the Christmas scene.

We made the most of Christmas at the homestead.

We started baking in early December, filling the air with the aroma of cinnamon and yeast. The table top was covered each evening with sweet round loaves and doughy shapes of Santas and stars waiting for frosting.

By the 15th, the tree had been cut from the woods, set up, and decorated with strings of cranberries picked that fall. To string and wind around the tree, we popped popcorn in iron pans on the wood-burning stove. Then the tinsel icicles were hung on the branches to brighten things up and the aluminum foil star was positioned on top like a crown.

Incoming Christmas cards were stapled to the rough lumber doors. The manger scene, lit with a battery-operated star, stood on the shelf, telling us the Christmas story each time we passed by.

Back on November evenings, the shopping had already been done, as we pored over the pages of the Sears catalog. Before Thanksgiving, the order had been sent out to be sure the packages would arrive in time for the big day.

On Christmas Eve, our very traditional family dined on red clam chowder, green-frosted Christmas Stollen, and home-made vanilla ice cream. After supper, Dad would read *A Christmas Carol* out loud. By the time Tiny Tim's turkey was delivered, our sleepy twins were ready to hang up their stockings and climb the ladder for bed.

But things didn't always go as smoothly as that. One year we lost the ice cream.

On the morning of Christmas Eve, I mixed up fresh eggs and goat's milk for the custard. Dad pulled icicles from the cabin roof into burlap bags, pounded them into little pieces with a hammer, and put them into the freezer tub with rock salt around the ice cream container. We took turns cranking the handle until it wouldn't move anymore — then Dad cranked it three more times. Taking out the paddle, he gave it to the kids to lick off, sealed the top of the container, covered it with more ice and several burlap bags, and put the whole thing out to ripen for a few hours.

That afternoon, we hauled wood from up the hill. When we returned, we found the freezer turned over, the burlap bags scattered, and the ice cream gone. One very fat and happy dog stood wagging his tail. Only our happy holiday spirit saved him from a grim end.

Undaunted, Dad went to get more icicles from the barn roof and we started all over again. This time the freezer was put out of the reach of marauders, and we finally did get to eat our dessert after the stockings were hung.

Another year, the packages we had ordered from Sears didn't arrive in Fairbanks on time. Sorry, they said at the catalog store, but they were behind in their shipments.

That Christmas Eve night, Dad and I sat up late, snipping pictures of the presents from the catalog, and putting them into envelopes strung up with red ribbon. We hung them on the door next to the Christmas cards with plaintive promises that the things would arrive before the New Year.

But Santa never really forgot us up there. After all, he was practically a neighbor! As we snuggled under our comforters, we were sure we heard the jingle of sleigh bells and the thumps of hoofbeats overhead.

At Christmastime, there was no better place to be than our homestead.

Moon Glow &
Northern Lights

AAAAAAAAAAAAAAAAAAAAAAAAAAAAAAAAAAAAAAAA

A laska is known as the Land of the Midnight Sun. Indeed, up in the Interior, we could read the paper outdoors at midnight in June.

Conversely, in mid-December, the sun barely rose over the horizon, and the nights were 20 hours long.

One would think that on a homestead far from the bright lights of town, those nights would be dark as pitch.

But that wasn't so.

Once snow was on the ground in the fall, it never really got black outside. The sky was full of stars that hung so close, we could almost reach up and touch them. The starlight reflected on the whiteness of the snow, and we could make out where we were going around the yard.

When the crescent moon started showing each month, its light outlined the trees around the house. As it grew bigger each night, shadows formed on the ground. When it came into the full, we didn't need lanterns or flashlights outside.

When the moon rose over the hill across the valley, it appeared to be 10 times its real size. It shone in the window, conspicuously, in our dimly lit cabin.

As it climbed up in the sky, making the silver birches and the white snow glisten, it made our yard look enchanted. It was lovely to be outdoors in the magical night. I would feel like a princess in a child's tale, surrounded by crystal castles in a fairyland.

Also in winter, the aurora borealis would put on a show in the sky. Whoever would spot them first called the rest of us outside. Sometimes we'd hear about them on the radio; the announcer would tell the listening audience, "The northern lights are out!"

Looking up from our yard, the lights were spectacular. Bright streaks extended from horizon to horizon, swirling and swooping across the sky. Turning red, green and purple, they changed shape and direction. Then, more bands of light would converge, and soon the whole sky was aflame. Overwhelming and magnificent, I'd swear I could hear them making swishing sounds.

The lights were remarkably brilliant.

One evening, while doing dishes, I looked out into the yard and thought, "My, the full moon is bright tonight." Then I remembered there had been a full moon two weeks before. The radiance was coming from the northern lights — the most beautiful show I had ever seen.

On some nights, the University of Alaska sent up rockets of barium to simulate the aurora from a launching site over on the Steese Highway. The radio would announce this, too, and we'd watch for the missile to zoom up into the sky with blue flames spouting from its tail. Up in the heavens it would explode, emitting a ring of bright colors that floated and expanded in a big arc. It was very pretty, but in a few minutes it would diffuse into the night.

Man's great efforts didn't hold a candle to nature's display.

The winter nights were long, but seldom dark. The luminous sky that lit up our homestead made the nights easier to bear and even enjoy.

Writing Home

W̲e loved our life on the homestead; we were as contented as could be. Never mind what others called hardships — cutting firewood, hauling water, dumping buckets — they didn't bother us. We were equal to the challenge. In fact, we took pride in finding more efficient ways to do those lowly chores.

So far from the nearest town, we had no power lines, no telephones, and no neighbors. In emergencies, we were on our own. But we were also independent and self-sufficient, and that meant a lot to us. Our homestead was a place that had long been dreamed of and finally attained.

But things took on a different light when I wrote letters home to Mom and Dad.

They lived, as we used to live, conservatively, with all the amenities of civilization that people simply take for granted. How could I explain what possessed us to throw away the good life, snatch up their grandchildren, and run off to a far north corner of the world?

I tried to tell them about homesteading and starting a new life: "We're carving a home out of the wilderness."

That sounded worthy of our efforts, if I left out some of the details.

I wrote about building a log cabin, hoping to conjure a vision of storybook pioneers. Each week, I'd recount the number of logs Dad had put up and how close we were to getting the roof on. But I didn't tell about working in the rain all day, or slapping at mosquitoes, or wondering how we'd scrape up the money for roofing materials.

I didn't want to spoil the image.

When I described our warm, cozy cabin with its pretty green chinking between the logs, I failed to mention how cold my poor fingers had been as I raced the winter winds, stuffing the moss into the cracks.

I told them that Dad had built me a fine kitchen counter with a formica top, but I omitted the fact that there was a six-gallon bucket under the sink. I wasn't trying to fool them; they knew we didn't have plumbing. There were just some things they didn't need to think about.

We lit our cabin with kerosene lamps and gaslights. Why not paint them picturesque instead of complaining about their dimness? I wanted so much to share with my folks my love for our cabin, our homestead, and Alaska. I had to make everything sound good, because, to me, everything was good.

When I wrote about our daily life, I tried to write about things they could relate to — like Sunday dinner, going for a winter walk in the moonlight, or going to town. I didn't tell how the roast was late because the green firewood wouldn't burn in the stove; that our moonlight walk was at three o'clock in the afternoon; or that it took an hour to heat up the truck engine with a weed burner! Instead, I wrote something like:

"We went to town to go Christmas shopping. Then we went to a nice restaurant for dinner. I wore the long red wool skirt you sent me, Mom." (Never mind about the long johns I wore underneath the skirt; or the long ride over the highway sitting four across in the cab of the pickup; or about the drums of gas and bags of feed that we bought along with the Christmas presents; or how we hurried through dinner so that the two weeks' supply of groceries left in the cab of the truck wouldn't freeze, and how we carried those same groceries home on our laps.)

Sometimes careful timing was necessary. There was no point in telling them when one of the kids had the flu, "Lanny is in bed with a temperature of 104 degrees." By the time the letter arrived at an alarmed Grandma and Grandpa's house, the sickness would be over and Lanny would be out playing and doing chores again. Better to say, "Lanny had a touch of the flu last week, but he's all better now."

Alaska and the East Coast seemed very far apart, and not just in physical distance. Our lifestyles were at opposite ends of the spectrum, too.

Even so, our life's goals and values were the same — home, family, and success in what we were doing. We faced challenges that would be hard for our parents to imagine, but we handled them the way we were brought up to do. There was a strong thread of unity between us, no matter how differently we lived, and our ties were never broken.

So, every week I sent letters to the folks back home with pretty word pictures about our homestead, hoping that they could somehow understand how much our life in Alaska meant to us.

Letter From My Screened-In Porch

Dear Folks,

    I'm sitting out on the screened-in porch with my cup of tea. Supper is over; the dishwater is heating over the last embers in the cookstove. Now that summer is coming, we'll be eating breakfast out here.

    The air is still, and the sun streams in the west windows onto my couch, inviting me to sit down. My couch is really the third seat of an old Travelall van Dad set on wooden blocks. Covered with a yellow-flowered throw, it fits just right at the end of the porch.

As I sip my tea, I look out over 100 stately birch trees just coming into leaf. Nailed to one is an aviary apartment house; three of the units have tenants — bright-colored swallows — peeking out from their quarter-size doors. This summer, they will keep our mosquito population down.

Out in the corral, Bree is nickering. Lanny must be coming with his can of horse chow; I hear the pellets rattle into the feed dish and Lanny's gentle talk.

Stirred up, the gander paces like a consort out in the yard, honking over the goose's back at every step, disturbing a pecking hen that squawks with indignation.

Black Eartha jumps up on my knee and starts her hourly bath. Finally satisfied, she turns around twice and settles down on my lap to purr. The tranquillity and solitude of my porch envelop me in contentment.

Not that it's always secluded like this. I recall 14 of us crowded together late one Labor Day evening, eating charcoaled London Broil, piles of green salad, and giant scoops of wild blueberry buckle. The red oil lamp glowed serenely on our dear friends' faces, and shadows flickered amiably matching our conversations.

In the winter this porch is also full, but of white-wrapped packages of frozen food, produce from our garden, baked goods from the kitchen, and sometimes moosemeat from a lucky hunting season. One year, a whole moose leg hung from the rafter, waiting unwrapped for Dad to saw chunks from whenever we wanted a pot roast dinner.

I feel chilly; the sun has passed behind the hill on its circular course around the summer sky. The geese have settled down in the front yard, their long necks stretching to hide their heads under their wings. Light strains of music drift down from

Dawn's tape player upstairs, and my kettle of water hums along, simmering.

Eartha jumps down, leaving a warm spot on my lap. I'll linger a few minutes, then follow her into the house. There is still much to do.

Love from all of us,

Joy

EPILOGUE

Times Change

▼▼▼▼▼▼▼▼▼▼▼▼▼▼▼▼▼▼▼▼▼▼▼▼▼▼▼▼▼▼▼▼▼▼▼▼

One day in 1975, a family with seven children drove up our driveway. They were looking for land on which to raise goats and chickens and still more children. Dad sold them the 40 acres across the road.

They, in turn, sold plots to other people and our solitary way of life was gone. Soon we were a neighborhood, conversing back and forth over CB radios, gathering together for potlucks and snowmobile parties, summer barbecues and barn-raisings. Our little schoolroom by the stove, which once held only a class of two, swelled with high school students.

But the biggest change of all came with the oil that was discovered on Alaska's North Slope. When pipeline construction began in earnest, our winding, peaceful Elliott Highway became a busy haul road. Each day, up to 300 trucks and equipment traveled by continuously.

By the time the twins were about grown and ready to go out on their own, we found ourselves in the midst of pipeline frenzy. More people stopped by wanting to buy land. We subdivided the clearing. A public school was built on the old potato patch.

As the youngsters in the big family across the road grew up, the parents adopted more children. They set up a business on their land, and called it "The Wildwood General Store at Joy, Alaska." Summer tour buses stop there on their way to Prudhoe Bay.

Dawn and Lanny went off to the University of Alaska in Fairbanks. Dawn studied food service, married, and had five children. In her spare time, she teaches sewing classes in her home. Lanny became an electrician and a Jack-of-all-trades. Like Dad, he can fix just about anything. Both he and Dawn still live in the Fairbanks area.

In 1980, after Dad reached retirement age, we moved 600 miles south to Homer, Alaska, and he built me a house with faucets, pipes, and everything automatic.

Then he set up shop downstairs where he builds furniture and toys. Each summer he builds a boat, usually some sort of classic small craft. Most recently he has been making wood and canvas canoes.

As for me, I worked as a substitute teacher at an elementary school in Homer until I, too, reached the age of retirement. Now I enjoy sitting at my state-of-the-art word processor, in my automatic house, writing about fond memories of our Home Sweet Homestead.

FROM ALASKA PRESS:

Alaska Pioneer Series:

HOME SWEET HOMESTEAD
by Joy Griffin
Sketches of Pioneer Life in Interior Alaska

THIS IS COFFEE POINT, GO AHEAD
by Wilma Williams
A Mother & Her Children Fish Bristol Bay, Alaska

IF YOU'VE GOT IT TO DO...
GET ON WITH IT
One Family's Life in Early Homer, Alaska

Alaska Landmark Series:

THE DAWG'S TALE
by Diane Ford Wood
The Story of the Salty Dawg Saloon,
The Homer Spit,
& The Town of Homer, Alaska

ALASKA PRESS
P.O. Box 90565-HSH
Anchorage, Alaska 99509-0565

To order, send $15.95 per book, plus $2.00 shipping/handling
(book rate) or $4.00 (priority mail) to Alaska Press.
Additional books will be shipped
for $1.00 (book rate) or $2.00 (priority mail).
Educational discounts and supplements are available.